THE WIT AND WISDOM

OF

STEPHEN KING

EDITED BY

ANDREW J. RAUSCH

BearManor Media

Albany, Georgia

The Wit and Wisdom of Stephen King
© 2011 Andrew J. Rausch.

Published in the USA by:
BearManor Media
PO Box 1129
Duncan, OK 73534-1129
www.BearManorMedia.com

ISBN 978-1-59393-648-8
ISBN-13: 978-1-59393-648-8

Printed in the United States.

Design and Layout by Allan T. Duffin.

This book is dedicated to Sherri Watson,
who gave me my first King book and
has always been supportive.

TABLE OF CONTENTS

INTRODUCTION

I was 11 years old in 1984, and popular culture already played a major role in my life. Hulk Hogan defeated the Iron Sheik to win his first World Wrestling Federation title belt that year, Michael Jackson's hair burst into flames during a Pepsi commercial shoot (being a huge fan of The Gloved One, I actually wept at this news), and *V* was both my favorite television series and comic book. But the one thing that stands out to me most about that year was my discovering a well-worn paperback copy of Stephen King's *Carrie* in the school library. Prior to this I had been reading and enjoying such varied authors as Jules Verne and Louis L'amour, but this guy Stephen King spoke to me in a way that no other writer had at this point.

King's colorful vernacular, the blue collar poetry of the everyman, was an eye-opener to be sure, but his main appeal was that he was describing things in a way that made sense to me; he was depicting the real and tangible world in which I lived. This was a world of Coca-Cola brand soft drinks, F-bombs, and real-life problems like peer pressure and teen depression. Rather than the fantastical worlds depicted by Verne or the idealized Old West of L'amour, King's characters seemed to live and breathe in the same podunk town I did. Hell, for all I knew, Carrie White and her batshit fundamentalist mother lived right down the street from me... The high school social class struggle that King described was just like that in my school and thousands of others. King himself has said that he feels distrust for people who say they actually enjoyed high school, implying that they were the tormentor rather than the tormentee, and that outlook serves as the foundation upon which *Carrie* was built. Like the novel's protagonist Carrie White, I was a bit of an outsider who dreamed of being one of the cool kids, so the novel held a certain resonance for me. I didn't have telekinesis, but don't think I didn't stand up and cheer like hell when Carrie got her revenge at the end of the novel. This is not to say that I would liked to have inflicted harm upon any of those oh-so-popular kids at my own school, but in that pre-Columbine world in which we knew where to draw the lines of fantasy, I loved the idea of the unpopular student—the nerd, if you will—exacting revenge in such a dramatic fashion.

I then read *Pet Sematary*, which scared the bejeezus out of me. I can actually remember shelving the book and declaring that I would not read another word of it. King's description of the decaying Victor Pascow had just been too vivid and detailed for my sixth-grade sensibilities. But then, predictably, I found myself lying in bed late at night, thinking about "Paxcow" and his ominous warnings to Louis Creed, and I came to the conclusion that I had to find out what happened next. And it was then, at about four in the morning, that I picked the book back up and resumed reading.

By this time I was certainly no stranger to the horror genre, but again there was something dramatically different about King's tales of the macabre that made them seem that much more frightening to me. Although I couldn't have put a finger on it at the time, the key difference between King and the horror that I had become accustomed to was the fact that he had taken the trappings of horror out of the Victorian castles and looming haunted houses and placed them right smack dab in the middle of my own living room. No longer were these horrors restricted to the fantastical monsters of Lovecraft or the poetic madmen of Poe; in the pages of King's novels, the horror was all around us. It was in our schools, our families, and our automobiles. Even the neighbor's lovable Saint Bernard was not beyond reproach. Certainly King was not the first writer to do this—authors like Robert Bloch and Richard Matheson had been doing this sort of thing for years—but through his gargantuan success King managed to singlehandedly change the direction and perception of the entire horror genre.

Like myself, millions of other readers were discovering King around this same time (from roughly 1980–1986), and he soon became one of the bestselling authors in the history of the printed word. In the mid-1980s, Stephen King was everywhere; you couldn't have thrown a rock without hitting a big-screen film adaptation of his work, the so-called Stephen King "novel of the month," or a magazine cover story about the man and his impact upon the publishing world and the genre in which he worked most frequently. Critics, suspicious of his successes, missed few opportunities to take swipes at the man and his work, constantly reminding us that King's novels were lowbrow and thus without merit. Despite this, legions of fans continued to gobble up everything

King published, from thrillers like *Misery* to the fantasy novel *The Eyes of the Dragon*. Soon a sub-genre of nonfiction emerged—books about Stephen King. The startling commercial success of books like Douglas Winter's *Stephen King: The Art of Darkness*, interview compilations such as *Bare Bones*, and even Stephen J. Spignesi's two Stephen King quiz books, established King as something of an anomaly; he was an author that readers found as fascinating as the novels he wrote.

King soon popped up in an American Express ad, solidifying his place as a modern day Hitchcock—the human personification of horror and suspense.

A documentary titled *Stephen King's World of Horror* then started airing on late night cable, and for a while it seemed like literally every other film that Hollywood released touted itself as being "from the mind of Stephen King." The author made us laugh with a memorable cameo in *Creepshow* ("Meteor shit!"), and we patiently waited for *Maximum Overdrive* to find out if King would be any good as a motion picture director. (Somehow I don't think King would take offense to my saying that he was no Stanley Kubrick.)

Stephen King was everywhere, and that trend has never really died out. He continued publishing a long succession of novels—generally at least one a year—as well as short story and novella collections and the occasional nonfiction work. A lot of us wept when we saw the moving King adaptations *Stand by Me* and *The Shawshank Redemption*, and maybe even more of us wept when Stephen King was nearly killed in an accident in the summer of 1999.

The thing is, for a lot of us, Stephen King has been one of the few constants throughout our lives. Popular athletes and even United States Presidents have come and gone like the flavor of the month, and yet Stephen King has stood the test of time, releasing serial novels, e-books, and even Kindle and audiobook exclusives. Maybe he isn't saturating the market in quite the same way he did 25 years ago, but Stephen King and his influence is all around us. For nearly a decade he has written about popular culture as a regular contributor to *Entertainment Weekly*, and has time and time again proven himself to be an astute analyst of entertainment trends and that absurd phenomenon known as celebrity behavior. Even when he's making ridiculous statements like "Samuel L. Jackson should have won an Oscar for *Lakeview Terrace*" we continue to tune in to find out what the man has to say.

For better or worse, Stephen King has become something of a voice for an entire generation, a sort of cross between the Hollywood pundits of programs like *Entertainment Tonight* and humorists like Mark Twain and Kurt Vonnegut. Whether he's talking about the horror genre that he himself has played such a tremendous role in reshaping and defining, or the role of organized religion in today's society, or even the qualitative aspects of HBO's now-defunct *The Wire*, Stephen King matters. What he has to say matters, and what he thinks matters, which is precisely why I felt that this volume was necessary. His commentaries and observations regarding his own life and work, as well as those about the world in which we live, are likely to be as important to his legacy as the hundreds of rich and incredible stories he's given us throughout his career.

Having said that, I should note that this volume cannot and should not be seen as a complete collection of every single quotation ever spoken by Stephen King that's worthy of collection. I pored over hundreds of interviews and essays and then chose what I felt was applicable. This process was, of course, hardly a scientific one; one hundred editors would likely have come up with one hundred different collections. It is, after all, subjective. Then there is that great big thousand pound elephant in the room, which I am about to draw even more attention to now, and that is the fact that it would be virtually impossible to locate every single interview that King has given since he first came to national attention in 1974. Because of this, no collection of King quotations can ever be said to be truly complete. Despite these limitations, I pressed forward diligently and compiled a collection of quotations that I feel is representative of the man, the writer, and the humorist that is Stephen King.

Enjoy.

§

FOREWORD
QUANTUM THEORY AND STEPHEN KING

BY TYSON BLUE

I've been reading a few diverse things as this foreword is being written, all of which seem to tie loosely together with the book you're holding in your hands and about to read when you finish this, if you haven't skipped over it and dived right in. And even if you're reading this, quantum theory says that there is an alternately universe coexisting simultaneously with this one where you did just that.

I've also read King's current new book, *Full Dark, No Stars*, but it's too early to talk about that just yet, and it's not really germane to this. But I digress...

One of the aforementioned diverse things, which actually put me in mind of the last paragraph, is Stephen Hawking's new book written with Leonard Mlodinow, *The Grand Design*, which posits a "theory of everything," which will tie together the natural and supernatural worlds without resort to super-stition. It basically states that every possible alternative universe exists at the same time, diverging at crucial intersections into infinite possible outcomes, which in turn spawn a multitude of possibilities of their own. Although mind-boggling to envision, it has an elegance about it which is endlessly fascinating.

I've also been reading *The Autobiography of Mark Twain, Vol. I*, which showed up, *UR*-like, on my Kindle a month ahead of its scheduled publication date. What ties Mark Twain to quantum theory, and ultimately to this book is Twain's notion of autobiography. Rather than starting at the beginning and working one's way forward to the present, Twain chose instead to write about portions of his life which interested him, in no particular order, theorizing that the story of his life would be told in the end, at least the interesting parts.

In both books, there are multiple threads twining around, intersecting at random and then moving on, perhaps to cross again later, perhaps not, but throughout a realm of infinite possibility. And that combination resonated with me when considering what I could say about this collection of random, albeit arbitrarily organized, quotes from Stephen King from all stages of his lengthy career.

Unlike Mr. Rausch, I can remember a time when there wasn't a Stephen King, or at least a published, world-famous author named Stephen King, since Steve was born before I was, and we were moving in circles that came fairly close, but hadn't intersected as yet.

We came close a couple of times. As I've said before in other places, I grew up in New England at about the same time as King. I lived in New Hampshire, while Steve lived in Maine. My father was the production manager for the northern division of a large textile firm called J.P. Stevens. One of the plants he managed was the Worumbo woolen and worsted plant in Lisbon Falls, Maine. Sometimes, when I had a day off from school, I would go along with him when he had to visit that plant, and spent some time wandering through the plant while he was busy. I'd also go up the hill from the plant to a small store that sold comics and magazines, and picked up some interesting things there from time to time.

I've often wondered if Stephen King, who was a high school student in Lisbon Falls at the same time, may have even been in there looking at some of the same things along with me. But there was a closer intersection than that, although I wasn't to learn about it until a few years ago.

One Saturday morning, I was reading an advance copy of *On Writing*, King's autobiographical guide to writing which remains one of the two or three best books ever written on the subject. I knew that he had worked one summer in a textile mill, an experience that resulted in the short story "Graveyard Shift." But I had no idea until that Saturday morning in Upstate New York that the plant he had worked in was the Worumbo plant. Reading that stopped me dead in my tracks.

Years before the publication of *Carrie* and all the worldwide fame that followed, and years before King and I met for the first time on the set of *Maximum Overdrive* in North Carolina on his birthday in 1985, Stephen King had briefly worked for my father.

How cool is that?

And my meetings with King have been like that, just coming together from time to time, at press conferences, movie sets, lectures, award ceremonies and so forth. The last time was a few years back, when I ran into him at Legal Sea Foods in Boston when we were both in town for a Red Sox–Yankees game.

And that's not unlike the experience you'll have reading this book. As you go through each chapter, you'll find out what King had to say on the subject, whether it's censorship, childhood, movies, money, media or writing, or any other of the thirty-two topics to be found herein. And you'll see what he had to say in the '70s, the '80s, etc., and how his insights and opinions on that particular topic have changed over the years.

And it's similar to Twain's model of autobiography, too, in that there is a lot of anecdotal life history in these pages, which give readers insight into how King has developed as a writer and a person over his career.

It actually calls to mind the line from "The Body," in which King writes that people move in and out of your life like busboys, which is a pretty apt analogy for most people these days. No one really stays in one place anymore. I grew up in New England, went to college in New York, then back to New Hampshire, then Georgia, and now am back in New York, hopefully for good.

The quotes collected here come from a wide variety of sources, from interviews for television, magazines or newspapers; from short pieces written for promotional materials for books or movies; from small literary journals like *The Paris Review* or from King's own website.

What Mr. Rausch has done here works on several levels. As a work of light autobiography, it provides a sort of Cliff's Notes version of King's life and work, hitting the high points in no particular order, but, if Twain is right, providing the essentials in a compact form.

The topical arrangement of the book lets readers who are searching for a pithy quote to spice up a term paper or essay with a plethora of great remarks for most occasions. Just remember to give the proper attribution when you use them…

This kind of book is also ideal for a quick read in situations where you don't have a lot of time to dive into a complicated story, such as during lunch breaks, sermons, political speeches, commercial breaks, while out for a walk, waiting for a doctor or dentist's appointment, or the classic trip to the bathroom.

It's also a nice introduction to King's skill as a raconteur, showing his skill at saying something interesting and insightful on a wide variety of subjects, giving people who might never get an opportunity to find out for themselves just how entertaining he is to kick back and talk with informally.

In other words, there are numerous ways in which you as a reader can approach this book, an almost infinite number of ways in which you can take the quotes herein. Some might inspire you to learn more about a particular topic, or give you an idea for a short story or a novel, or for a screenplay. When I try to trace back the beginnings of the path that took me from reading a paperback copy of *Carrie* in the mid-'70s to standing in a prison death-house that had existed only in King's mind along with a group of world-class talent, my head starts to hurt. And that's not even counting the choices of books, movies and comics and life experiences that shape me into the person who wanted to read King's work in the first place.

I guess what I'm trying to say here is that almost everything in life can take you in countless directions, too many to count, and a book like this is the kind of random collection of loosely-organized snippets which forms, at least to me, ideal fuel for a quest that can take you almost anywhere.

It's not a book I ever would have thought of putting together—the closest I ever came was a piece I did for Jim Steranko's *Mediascene* back in the mid-'70's, where I "interviewed" Robert E. Howard's *Conan the Barbarian* by taking actual quotes from Conan from Howard's original stories and crafting questions to which they would work as answers. That was my take on using quotes—although the idea, as I recall, was Steranko's, to give credit where it's due... But this book is Andy Rausch's response to that idea, each shaped by our own interests and ideas, and going off in completely different directions.

And who knows where it will take you? The only way to find out is to get started.

—*Walworth, New York*
October 15, 2010

§

Tyson Blue is the author of the non-fiction works The Unseen King, Observations From the Terminator, Walking the Mile: The Making of The Green Mile *and the novel* Season of the Gun. *He served as Contributing Editor for* Castle Rock: The Stephen King Newsletter *from 1985-1989, and in the same capacity for* Cemetery Dance *from 1992-1999. His blog, "Needful Kings and Other Things", appears online from time to time.*

The Wit and Wisdom of Stephen King

CENSORSHIP

"The issue behind censorship is always somebody saying, 'My point of view is more valid than your point of view.' If the censorship initiative succeeds, then the answer is, 'Yes, my views are more valid than your views; my views are more moral than your views.'"
　　　　　—*War of Words*, 1993

"[F]or a lot of conservatives and fundamentalists, there is a point on the blade of democracy where that double edge becomes a single edge; and that point always occurs when their own personal sensibilities are offended."
　　　　　—Lecture at Virginia Beach, September 22, 1986

"As a nation, we've been through too many fights to preserve our rights of free thought to let them go just because some prude with a highlighter doesn't approve of them."
　　　　　—*Bangor Daily News*, March 20, 1992

"I was involved with an anti-obscenity referendum in Maine. The referendum question was very simply stated: 'Do you want to make it a crime to sell or vend obscene material?' This is sort of like saying, 'Do you want to make it a crime to kill Santa Claus?'"
　　　　　—Lecture at Virginia Beach, September 22, 1986

"[Jerry] Falwell says that sex books like *Penthouse* should be taken off the lower racks, where little children can look at depravity and barnyard sex acts and words and all this other stuff. Of course, he's standing up there on TV saying

this, and never in my life have I ever seen a *Penthouse* magazine down there where the three- or four- or five-year-olds could grab it off the shelf."
—*Penthouse*, April 1982

"You know how impressionable teenagers are. They can't be trusted to do anything; they are totally useless human beings who will do anything their friends tell them to do—give them Golden Books and they'll grow up to be responsible adults capable of facing the world..."
—Lecture at Virginia Beach, September 22, 1986

"I don't believe that John Wayne Gacy, in Chicago, did what he did because he read a novel—or Juan Corona, or Ted Bundy. It's built in."
—*West Magazine*, July 19, 1987

"I have no problem with that at all, if they take *Cujo* or *Salem's Lot* or *The Shining* out of a public school.... I would just say to you as students who are supposed to be learning, that as soon as that book is gone from the library, do not walk—run to your nearest public library or bookseller and find out what your elders don't want you to know, because that's what you need to know! Don't let them bullshit you and don't let them guide your mind, because once it starts, it never stops. Some of our most famous leaders have been book-banners, like Hitler, Stalin, Idi Amin."
—Lecture at Virginia Beach, September 22, 1986

"That's what's always down the road when you begin to censor—Crystal Night."
[Editor's note: "Crystal Night," or *Kristallnacht*, was an infamous night in 1939 when the Nazis burned all literature that they deemed subversive.]
—*Omni*, 1987

"If you are not careful and diligent about defending the right of your children to read, there won't be much left, especially at the junior-high level where kids really begin to develop a lively life of the mind, but books about heroic boys who come off the bench to hit home runs in the bottom of the ninth and shy girls with good personalities who finally get that big prom date with the boy of their dreams. Is this what you want for your kids, keeping in mind that controversy and surprise—sometimes even shock—are often the whetstone on which young minds are shaped?"
—*The Bangor Daily News*, March 20, 1992

"Do I think that all books and all ideas should be allowed in school libraries? I do not. Schools are, after all, a 'managed' marketplace. Books like *Fanny Hill* and Brett Easton Ellis' gruesome *American Psycho* have a right to be read by people who want to read them, but they don't belong in the libraries of tax-supported American middle schools. Do I think that I have an obligation to fly down to Florida and argue that my books, which are a long way from either *Fanny Hill* or *American Psycho*, be replaced on the shelves from which they have been taken? No. My job is writing stories, and if I spent all my time defending the ones I've written already, I'd have no time to write new ones."

—*The Bangor Daily News*, March 20, 1992

§

CHILDHOOD

"Now why are we on my childhood? Could it be you think I'm...well...a little strange? Actually I had a very normal childhood. There was the cannibalism, of course, but..."
　　　—AOL chat, October 10, 2000

"Let's stop right here and just say, whenever an interviewer says, 'So, when you were a kid...,' what they're doing is basically saying, 'What screwed you up so bad that you're doing what you're doing now?' Nothing happened. I didn't used to light fires when I was a kid, anything like that."
　　　—*60 Minutes*, February 16, 1997

"You can remember things about your childhood, but I've come to the conclusion that most of the things that we remember about our childhood are lies. We can have dreams where we redream things that are truer than what we remember waking. We all have memories that stand out from when we were kids, but they're really just snapshots. You can't remember how you reacted because your whole head is different when you stand aside."
　　　—*High Times*, January 1981

"I had a very innocent childhood. Very bucolic. I grew up in a small town. Innocence would describe it. No drugs, no needles, no gang fights. It was a big deal for us if our parents were out and we could play spin the bottle with the girls. Put a few records on. The Sting Rays would play Saturday nights at the Grange Hall."
　　　—*The Guardian*, September 14, 2000

"We were raised by my mother, who was a single mom, so we were latch key kids in the Fifties before latch key kids actually existed. So in that sense there was no dad around."
—*Nightline*, November 15, 2007

"[I]t was a classic desertion, not even a note of explanation or justification left behind. [My father] said, literally, that he was going out to the grocery store for a pack of cigarettes, and he didn't take any of his things with him. That was in 1949, and none of us have heard from the bastard since."
—*Playboy*, June 1983

"I came home one day and my mother was absolutely white. 'I think I've just seen your father on the news,' she said. It was when there was all the fighting in the Congo in the Sixties and she thought he was one of a bunch of mercenaries. Maybe that's how he ended up."
—*Toronto Star*, October 5, 1983

"No, I don't hate [my father]. Maybe if I had him around now, and he wasn't really just totally decrepit, I'd kick his ass for him a couple of times."
—*60 Minutes*, February 16, 1997

"[W]e knocked around a lot of places, because my mom would get a job, and then either she'd lose it, because she got laid off, or something would happen, or the babysitter wouldn't show up, and my brother, who was two years older, is the babysitter, and somebody would see him crawling around on the roof of the apartment building after his ball, and we'd get evicted from that place, and we'd go somewhere else."
—*Nightline*, November 15, 2007

"She worked at a succession of low-paying jobs: presser in a laundry, doughnut-maker on the night shift at a bakery, store clerk, housekeeper. She was a talented pianist and a woman with a great and sometimes eccentric sense of humor, and somehow she kept things together, as women before her have done and as other women are doing even now as we speak."
—*Danse Macabre*, 1981

"My nightmares as a kid were always inadequacy dreams. Dreams of standing up to salute the flag and having my pants fall down."
—*Yankee*, March 1979

"As a small boy, I was convinced that all those big trucks—the semis, the 18-wheelers—were hungry for boy meat. And it didn't matter whether they were idling, running or stopped. They just scared the devil out of me."
—*Orange Coast Magazine*, November 1986

"When I was a kid I believed everything I was told, everything I read, and every dispatch sent out by my own overheated imagination. This made for more than a few sleepless nights, but it also filled the world I lived in with colors and textures I would not have traded for a lifetime of restful nights."
—*Nightmares & Dreamscapes* (Introduction), 1992

"I was terrified and fascinated by death—death in general and my own in particular—probably as a result of listening to all those radio shows as a kid and watching some pretty violent TV shows, such as *Peter Gunn* and *Highway Patrol*, in which death came cheap and fast. I was absolutely convinced that I'd never live to reach twenty."
—*Playboy*, June 1983

"I used to have a scrapbook as a kid with this picture of a famous mass murderer in it. When my mother found my scrapbook with pictures of Charles Starkweather, she said, 'Good God, you're warped.'"
—*Sounds*, May 21, 1983

"And I said to my mother, 'I'm studying [Starkweather's] face so I'll know it if I see it, and know to get out of that person's way.' … And you could see it in his eyes, to a degree. There was something gone in there. But I also understood that was in me, and it was in a lot of people."
—*60 Minutes*, February 16, 1997

"As a kid growing up in rural Maine, my interest in horror and the fantastic wasn't looked upon with any approval whatsoever—there went young Steve King, his nose either in a lurid issue of *Tales from the Vault* or an even more lurid paperback of some sort or other—I had gone from Robert Bloch to Frank Belknap Long and from Long to the rest of the so-called Lovecraft Circle. I was, as far as most of my elders were concerned, eating tomatoes…poison fruit."
—*Mr. Monster's Movie Gold* (Introduction), 1986

"I wasn't the kind of kid who would get elected to student council, but neither did I lurk around the lockers looking like I was just waiting for somebody to haul off on me."
—*Famous Monsters*, April 1980

"I was never socially inarticulate. Not a loner. And that saved my life, saved my sanity. That and the writing. But to this day I distrust anybody who thought high school was a good time. Anybody. You can be happy at eight or even at 28. But if you say you were happy at 16, I'd say you were a fucking liar, or you were abnormal, disturbed…"
—*The Guardian*, September 14, 2000

"Let's face it. No kid in high school feels as though they fit in. The smartest thing that I ever heard anybody say about high school was that, 'If you look back upon that as the happiest time of your life, I don't want to know you.' High school was not the happiest time of my life, but I fit in."
—*Nightline*, November 15, 2007

"I graduated I think something like 17th in a class of about 190 or something like that. I was not number one in my class or number two or anything like that. I was not a total dip either. I got in trouble off and on because I wrote things about teachers or something like that and so I did standard number of detention halls and stuff like that."
—*Inside*, April 4, 1986

"I could write, and that was the way I defined myself, even as a kid."
—*Dream Makers: Volume II*, 1983

§

CRITICS

"A lot of critics see blood and say we're turning the country into a bunch of mongrel dogs that are running for blood. What a pile of bullshit that is!"
   —*Penthouse*, April 1982

"[T]here are some critics who write reviews that say, 'This stuff is crap.' It may be 'dangerous crap' or 'pulp' to them, but on the whole I think as far as any judgment goes, the only thing that matters is what I think of it."
   —*Sounds*, May 21, 1983

"That little elite, which is clustered in the literary magazines and book-review sections of influential newspaper magazines on both coasts, assumes that all popular literature must also, by definition, be bad literature. Those critics are not really against bad writing; they're against an entire type of writing. My type of writing, as it turns out. Those avatars of high culture hold it almost as an article of religious faith that plot and story must be subordinated to style, whereas my deeply held conviction is that story must be paramount..."
   —*Playboy*, June 1983

"We're talking about 'they,' and who I mean by 'they,' generally speaking, are the self-appointed guardians of literature, who a lot of times, turn out to be critics. Not always. But they're the people who really feel it would be better for my readers to watch television, because they're corrupting the word pool."
   —*Fangoria*, April 1984

"There's an innate selfishness in the idea for the intelligentsia, where they say, 'We're not even going to try to bring good literature to the majority of the American reading public, because it's useless. They're so stupid, it's useless.' That kind of elitism drove me totally insane as a younger man. And I'm better now, but there's still a fair amount of resentment toward that."
—*Nightline*, November 15, 2007

"There was a time when the idea of criticism was to make the writer a better writer, as well as to perform a consumer service for the reader. I think criticism should still fulfill that, although it does that less and less."
—*WB #145*, 1987

"Critics and scholars have always been suspicious of popular success. Often their suspicions are justified. In other cases, these suspicions are used as an excuse not to think."
—*On Writing*, 2000

"Earlier in my career, I was just excoriated by the critics. I was just drubbed un-mercifully, and I think I got more of it because the books were successful, and they were just horrified because they sensed it was something that was working in the popular context. It was different than what had gone before. And the thing they settled on was the brand names [that appeared in my work]. There was review after review that said this can't be up to anything serious because it's so ephemeral, because he's talking about Excedrin, he's talking about Pres-tone antifreeze, whatever it was. What they never took into consideration was that there was a whole generation, a huge generation, suckled on television."
—*Writer's Digest*, March 1992

"The final message of too many self-anointed critical smarties, whether stated or implied, seems to be, We don't really need to read this stuff to know it's junk, do we? ... Tom Wolfe was right when he exhorted novelists 15 years ago to reclaim American fiction from self-centered postmodernists who seem to actively scorn anything resembling an actual plot. It's those writers—not to mention critics who'd be ashamed to be seen in public with a Tony Hillerman mystery—who are strangling the novel and ceding a rich and fertile country of the imagination to the overt imagists who make the movies and television shows. There's nothing wrong with movies and TV, but there's also nothing

wrong with the sort of books Tom Wolfe hoped would describe 'this wild, bizarre, unpredictable, Hog-stomping Baroque country of ours.'"
—*Entertainment Weekly*, January 21, 2005

"It's my culture and I love it dearly—I have, I think, ever since the age of 8, in a Connecticut movie theater, when I first heard Clark Gable tell Vivien Leigh, "Frankly, my dear, I don't give a damn." There are plenty of people who see this beautiful junkshop carnival as lowbrow, thoughtless, ruinous, even vicious (I'm thinking of folks like Harold Bloom, the literary critic who had a cow when the National Book Foundation gave me an award for, ahem, Distinguished Contribution to American Letters). They are not, as a rule, the ones who shoot off fireworks on the Fourth of July. Or subscribe to *Entertainment Weekly*, for that matter. Many are folks who believe art should be work and see entertainment as subversive."
—*Entertainment Weekly*, July 29, 2005

"The problem, I think, is that there's almost no understanding in the serious critical establishment, and when I say that, I mean in the journals—everything from Harold Bloom to *Ploughshares* to—pick your poison, the *Antioch Review*, etc. I read these things. Do the people who publish them read me? That's a good question. If they do, a lot of them probably don't admit it. If their literary friends come over, they might put my books under the bed like…lit-porn. You people may have faced this; some friends will come over and say, ' Oh, you read him? Really? You read Stephen King? Well, all righty. Guess we won't be coming here again."
—Q&A in Portland, Oregon, November 2, 2006

"You know, you read critics who say, 'He could publish his laundry list,' but I don't think it'd be a best-seller. Nobody would want to read about how many shorts and how many shirts need starch."
—*Larry King Live*, April 10, 1986

"Since 1980 or so, some critics have been saying I could publish my laundry list and sell a million copies or so, but these are for the most part critics who think that's what I've been doing all along."
—*Nightmares & Dreamscapes* (Introduction), 1992

"I read my reviews fairly closely and get depressed by the bad ones, but on only two or three occasions have really awful write-ups interfered with my lunch."
—*Cosmopolitan*, December 1985

"In many ways, Eula-Beulah prepared me for literary criticism. After having a two-hundred-pound babysitter fart on your face and yell Pow!, *The Village Voice* holds few terrors."
—*On Writing*, 2000

"Of course I care about reviews, and any writer or creative person who says he doesn't is a goddamn liar. And secondly, if they are really disregarding what the critics say, they are making a terrible mistake."
—*Knave*, 1987

"The worst advice? 'Don't listen to the critics.' I think that you really ought to listen to the critics, because sometimes they're telling you that something is broken that you can fix. I think the advice 'Don't listen to the critics' is a sort of defensive thing that says if you stick your head in the sand, you won't have to hear any bad news and you won't have to see any bad news and you won't have to change what you're doing. But if you listen, sometimes you can get rid of a bad habit. And hey, critics...none of us like 'em, but if they're all saying something's a piece of shit, they're right."
—*Writer's Digest*, March 1992

§

DIRECTING
MAXIMUM OVERDRIVE

"One of the reasons I've committed myself to being here so extensively for the production of *Creepshow* is that I'd like to direct something myself one day. I don't want to make it my career or my life, but I'd like to do it once, because I see things in horror films and I say, 'I could do better than that.'"
—*Cinefantastique*, September-October 1982

"The reason that I [directed] it was because for years, people have said to me that the movies don't carry the spirit of the books. ... [S]o I thought, if I do it one time, now it may come out, and the critics might say, 'Guess what, Stephen King can't do Stephen King either!'"
—*Larry King Live*, April 10, 1986

"I went in and did *Maximum Overdrive*. Yeah, mostly to find out if it would work because so many people have said, 'I just don't go anymore. It's not you and that's it.'"
—*Fangoria*, August 1986

"Besides a certain freak show value, I imagine [producer Dino De Laurentiis] thought people would come for the same reason as Samuel Johnson said that people would come to see women preachers and dancing dogs. You don't expect to see it done well, you pay to see it done at all. So I think a lot of people will come just to see, you know, how bad I fucked up."
—*Boston Herald*, July 27, 1986

"I never asked what the budget was, and Dino [De Laurentiis] never told me. I knew what I wanted, and he said, 'I'll support you.' I said, 'Do you give me your word?' And he said, 'I give you my word.' And I went out and I shot the picture. I got everything I wanted. I think we spent maybe four million bucks; it wasn't a big budget at all. We finished under schedule; we finished under budget."
    —*Prevue*, May-July 1986

"You have to listen [to input] because everybody on the set has made more movies than you have. And that holds true for Steven Spielberg, who's probably got grips, techs, lighting guys who have made like 250 pictures, who have forgotten things that he'll never learn."
    —*Chicago Sun-Times*, July 1986

"[Making a movie] is a very primitive way to create. Eighty people standing around with their thumbs up their ass drinking Gatorade because the sun's behind a cloud is a primitive way to create."
    —*Maine Times*, July 11, 1986

"I got paid $70,000 to direct this thing, and as far as I'm concerned it was disaster pay. This whole business is so...unreal."
    —*San Francisco Chronicle*, July 22, 1986

"I think [*Maxium Overdrive* is] pretty good! I don't think that it's—I'm not rehearsing my Academy Award speech. It does what I want it to do; I mean, it's a dumb summer picture, so what?"
    —*Boston Herald*, July 27, 1986

"It's a stupid movie in a way—it's a chicken circuit movie. I thought it was hilarious when the guy was farting in the bathroom, and I took more critical chewing about that. I don't know what's wrong with people these days! It seems like nobody wants to laugh at anything unless it's Woody Allen!"
    —*Feast of Fear*, 1989

"Did you see *White Nights*? The difference between the movie Reiner made [*Stand by Me*] and the movie I made is like the difference between Baryshnikov and Gregory Hines. I can tap dance."
    —*Chicago Sun-Times*, July 1986

§

Early Works

"The earliest writing I can remember doing is when I was stuck in bed with the flu and started copying Tom Swift books into a tablet, changing the stories as I went along. Once you get a taste of that kind of power, you're lost forever."
—*Milwaukee Journal*, September 15, 1980

"Believe it or not, I was about six or seven, just copying panels out of comic books and then making up my own stories."
—*The Paris Review*, Fall 2006

"I started to submit [stories to magazines] when I was twelve, and obviously at that time they weren't good enough, and I suppose in my heart of hearts I knew it. But you have to start sooner or later, you have to dig in."
—"An Evening with Stephen King at the Billerica," 1983

"I started to submit stuff when I was about twelve, to magazines like *Fantastic* or *Fantasy and Science Fiction*. These stories had the trappings of science fiction, they were set in outer space, but they were really horror stories."
—*Dream Makers: Volume II*, 1983

"The first story I ever had published appeared in a fanzine published by Marv Wolfman, who now writes for the comics. It was called 'In A Half World of Terror,' and I have a copy of it somewhere. That goes back to my Sophomore year of high school, which would have been 1964."
—*Famous Monsters*, April 1980

"I wrote a novel at 16. I wrote another one that was a little better at 19 and another at 20. When I was 22, I wrote one that nearly got published."
        —*Milwaukee Journal*, September 15, 1980

"[T]he first four novels that I wrote, beginning at age 16, went unpublished. I became a published writer in the pulp jungle… I began at age 18 publishing a story in a magazine called *The Magazine of Strange Tales*, which was one of the last of the pulp magazines, for $35. I worked my way up to those magazines, which, if you hold them up horizontally, the gatefold would fall out."
        —*Nightline*, January 13, 1984

"I tried once to write a porn novel when I was in college eating fried Cheerios—I just couldn't do it. I mean, I did about 50 pages and I just said, 'Fuck, I can't do this.' The words were there, but I couldn't handle it. I just collapsed. It was so weird. I got to the point where the twin sisters are making love in the bird bath and I just said, 'I'm sorry…'"
        —*Interview*, January 1986

"Just before I got married in 1970, I sold a story to [*Cavalier*], and another, from then on I could sell them almost anything. I tried to sell them a story about a corpse that came back to life, but Nye Willden, the editor, said the corpse would have moldered away after a hundred years. I thought that was a really nasty quibble."
        —*Twilight Zone*, April 1981

"So I published a lot of stories in *Cavalier* and *Dude* and *Gent*. I published one in *Adam* that I wish was not under my real name, but it was, 'cause that's a real sleezo magazine."
        —"Probabilities," September 8, 1979

"This is no bullshit: any medical treatment for my kids' childhood diseases was paid for by mags with titles like *Cavalier* and *Dude*. Oh, and *Juggs*. That's charming, isn't it? Naked women paid for my kids' health."
        —Interview with Ben Rawortit, date unknown

"I never got to the point where I was publishing in magazines like *Big Buns* or anything like that, but I published in a lot of sleazy magazines."
        —*Orange Coast Magazine*, November 1986

"We were living in a trailer on top of a bleak, snowswept hillside in Hermon, Maine, which, if not the asshole of the universe, is at least within farting distance of it. I'd come home exhausted from school and squat in the trailer's furnace room, with Tabby's little Olivetti portable perched on a child's desk I had to balance on my knees, and try to hammer out some scintillating prose."
—*Playboy*, June 1983

"When I got out of college I couldn't get a teaching job. I pumped gas, I worked in another mill, I worked in an industrial laundry, and I'd go to the library and I'd get a book and I'd open it up and in the front I would see something like, 'The author would like to thank the Nathaniel Guggenhiem Foundation for the money to write...' and I'd think, 'you fucking shithead, where do you get off taking that money so you can sit on your ass in some cabin in New Hampshire while I'm trying to write a book at night and I've got bleach burns all over my hands. Who the fuck are you?'"
—*Miami Herald*, March 25, 1984

"From a financial point of view, two kids were probably two too many for college grads working in a laundry and the second shift at Dunkin' Donuts. The only edge we had came courtesy of magazines like *Dude, Cavalier, Adam*, and *Swank*—what my Uncle Oren used to call 'the titty books.' By 1972 they were showing quite a lot more than bare breasts and fiction was on its way out, but I was lucky enough to ride the last wave."
—*On Writing*, 2000

"I did a race riot novel, *Sword of the Darkness*, that was just terrible. After that I started to get it together; I did *Carrie* and *Salem's Lot*, and the other stuff came right along."
—*Starship*, Spring 1981

§

FAME

"I'm very leery of thinking that I'm somebody. Because nobody really is. Everybody is able to do something well, but in this country there's a premium put on stardom. An actor gets it, and a writer gets it."
—*Yankee*, March 1979

"I'm a little amazed by the whole thing, and I don't really understand it. Writers are not stars; they're not supposed to be stars."
—*Famous Monsters*, April 1980

"One of the odd things that happens about being famous is that you learn to always button your fly or to zip it because people say, 'That's Stephen King and his fly's undone!' Which is always a good time."
—Lecture at Virginia Beach, September 22, 1986

"You discover, little by little, that if you are a cultural phenomenon, or if you're a celebrity—and I don't know if I'm a cultural phenomenon, but I know I'm a celebrity—but in America, that's like…hot dogs. It doesn't really mean anything in a wider sense. Orson Bean is a celebrity. Charles Nelson Reilly is a celebrity. I watched this guy on *Hollywood Squares* for about seven years, and one day, my kid said to me, 'But what does he do?' And I said, 'I don't know.' I don't know what Charles Nelson Reilly did."
—*Fangoria*, April 1984

"The apotheosis of real pop culture celebrity was finally reached last week when someone called from Merv Griffin with an offer to do either *Hollywood Squares* or *The $10,000 Pyramid*. The medium is the message all right, but with a writer that's just not the way God intended it."
—*Maine Times*, July 11, 1986

"You know, I've got three kids and I've changed all their diapers in the middle of the night, and when it's two o'clock in the morning and you're changing something that's sort of special delivery with one eye open and one eye shut you don't feel famous. And I live in Bangor, Maine, which is not a town calculated to make anybody feel famous."
—"An Evening with Stephen King at the Billerica," 1983

"Writers, novelists in particular, are actually supposed to be secret agents. We're supposed to be observers, but not observed."
—ABA speech, June 2, 1991

"Life's a banquet for celebs; your waiter will gladly settle for an autograph instead of a tip. (Especially since he can sell it on eBay for big bucks, if he's ever really hard up.) But there is a price to be paid. ... Eat all you want, sure. But all too often you get to the end of the meal and discover that you're for dessert."
—*Entertainment Weekly*, October 24, 2003

"Being famous sucks. There is no upside. The downside is when you realize that the only reason everything on the buffet is free is because they're planning on having you for dessert."
—*Mystery Scene*, 1987

"We make a business here, apparently, of dining upon the bodies of those who have given us the most pleasure and some of our fondest memories; first we lionize them, and then we eat them."
—*Bangor Daily News*, December 13-14, 1980

"You discover, little by little, that everybody was right; that a lot of people will come on to you, and it turns out that there's a bottom line that they want something."
—*Fangoria*, April 1984

"I'm more wary of new acquaintances than I would be if I was not 'famous.' When people call me up, the first thought that flashes through my mind now isn't, 'How nice it is to hear from this person,' but 'What does he want?'"
—*Cosmopolitan*, December 1985

"Let's get one thing straight, okay? In that strange, vulgar, brightly colored section of the popular culture known as Celebrity World, the paparazzi are the lowest form of human life. I have been touched by them only peripherally, and it's been years since I really engaged their flea-like attention, yet recalling their exuberant shouts—'Hey, Stephen, look over here! Stephen, just one more! Hey, Stephen, where ya goin'?'—is still enough to make my skin prickle with shame and fury. The intrusion is part of it, the sense of entitlement is more of it, but the constant bray of your first name is the worst of it. They use your first name the way cops on *The Shield* do when they're interviewing child molesters."
—*Entertainment Weekly*, July 14, 2006

"And there was no happily ever after [in the story of Anna Nicole Smith]—except for the celebrity mags, tabloids, and cable-TV franchises that subsist on gossip and feast on death. Those guys had a ball, and the party will continue in the weeks ahead. As I said, this is a fairy tale we all know, and this seems to be the ending we most…like? No, I won't believe that, I refuse to believe we actually like such endings, but it is the one we most readily understand. Maybe there's a part of us that thinks famous people, especially the pretty ones, are like Icarus with his wax and feather wings: doomed to fly too close to the sun and go tumbling down. And maybe, in our secret hearts, we think they deserve to go tumbling down."
—*Entertainment Weekly*, February 23, 2007

"Bruce Springsteen reached into his pocket and took out the pen, but she never even looked at the guy. She [looked at me and] said, 'Aren't you Stephen King? I've read everything you ever wrote!'"
—ABA speech, June 2, 1991

"When you're famous, everybody accuses you of everything, from petty theft to the murder of John Lennon."
—*Entertainment Weekly*, July 10, 2009

§

FAMILY

"I spend a lot of time parenting because I'm home. A friend of mine told me that the average father sees each kid an average of twenty-two minutes a week, which I found almost unbelievable. Mine are in my hip pocket all the time. And I like it that way."

—High Times, January 1981

"To me the real purpose of having kids has nothing to do with perpetuating the race or the survival imperative. Rather, it's the way of finishing off your own childhood... By having children you're able to re-experience everything you experienced as a child, only from a more mature perspective."

—Parents Magazine, January 1982

"Around the house, he knows I'm daddy. When I leave on a trip like this, he says, I'm going off to be Stephen King."

—Milwaukee Journal, September 15, 1980

"I ended up writing a lot of books about fatherhood to try and understand it better. Because in some ways that's what fiction writers do. We write to try and figure out how we feel about certain things. *The Shining*, for instance, with the homicidal father; I had feelings of anger about my kids that I never expected. I had never been led to believe by sitcom TV, or movies like *It's a Wonderful Life* that it was ever possible to think, 'Won't this darned kid ever go to bed and let me write?' And Jack Torrance came out of that experience—an attempt to understand that experience."

—Nightline, November 15, 2007

"I thought I knew what a dad was. Fathers on TV were always cool. They had it together. Dad even wore a tie to the dinner table. The first time I realized that parents are not always good was when the kid wouldn't stop crying in the middle of the night. I was getting up to get the kid a bottle, and somewhere in the back of my mind, in some sewer back there, an alligator stirs... Make it stop crying. You know how to do it—use the pillow."
—Speech in Pasadena, California, 1982

"I think that I wrote about the relationship between kids and adults, kids and parents for a long time because I was trying to understand my own childhood and also because I had small children."
—*Boston Herald*, July 27, 1986

"So I didn't know KC and the Sunshine Band, but I did know my kids inside out. I was in touch with the anger and exhaustion that you can feel. And those things went into the books because they were what I knew at that time. What has found its way into a lot of the recent books is pain, and people who have injuries, because that's what I know right now. Ten years from now maybe it will be something else, if I'm still around."
—*The Paris Review*, Fall 2006

"Well, the kids grew up and the kids were okay. I never wrote anything about children out of sadism or a sense of anger. It was more like, if I write this, it won't happen. It was a kind of trying to keep the hex off."
—*The Times*, October 21, 2006

"I knew that Tabby was my ideal reader from the first time that I gave her something to read, before we were married, which was a story called 'I Am the Doorway' that's in my first collection, *Night Shift*. She said, 'This is really good.' And that's usually the extent of her comments, if she likes something. She will line-edit, and she will always tell me if she thinks something really sucks. She'll say, 'This is terrible.'"
—Q&A in Portland, Oregon, November 2, 2006

"Whenever I see a first novel dedicated to a wife (or a husband), I smile and think, There's someone who knows. Writing is a lonely job. Having someone who believes in you makes a lot of difference. They don't have to make speeches, just believing is usually enough."
—*On Writing*, 2000

Fans and Fan Mail

"I'll tell you the truth: A lot of [the fan mail] I don't read because it's repetitive and a little bit scary. If you think too much about [writing]…it's like being an actor on the stage. It's all right to know the audience is there; it's all right to sense them as a bulk presence, but never look for faces. They're out there and that's enough. I can't look them in the eye, one by one. It's scary. It's like what I do is very un-selfconscious. I do it for myself, because if you don't like it yourself, if you don't write for yourself, if you write for some hypothetical audience, it's not good—it's fake."

—*The Stephen King Companion*, 1989

"I'm still a fan at heart and one of the things which is real tough is not being able to go to a convention and go into the huckster's room and look around, maybe pick up some copies of *Weird Tales* or other pulps without having people come for autographs, or to talk about something they've written, or you've written. They're hitting on you all the time and you try to be polite and you try to talk to them but often you are just thinking to yourself, 'Why can't I be like these other people and just be allowed to browse?' You've become the browsee instead of the browser, kind of like a walking, talking book."

—*Knave*, 1987

"I don't think I have ever met Annie Wilkes [of *Misery*] yet, but I've met all sorts of people who call themselves my 'number-one fan' and, boy, some of [them] don't have six cans in a six-pack."

—Speech in Pasadena, California, date unknown

"He said, 'What do you think of your fans?' and I said, 'Well, they're sort of like me. They're sort of warped—that's why they like this stuff.'"
—"An Evening with Stephen King at the Billerica," 1983

"I have been asked if I beat my children and/or my wife. I have been asked to parties in places I have never been and hope never to go. I was once asked to give away the bride at a wedding, and one young woman sent me an ounce of pot, with the attached question: 'This is where I get my inspiration—where do you get yours?'"
—"'Ever Et Raw Meat?' and Other Weird Questions," 1987

"The lunatic fringe is less than one percent. It's a rare week when we find [such a letter]. We just sort of all gather together and exclaim over it."
—*Fangoria*, April 1984

"Do I mind these questions? Yes…and no. Anyone minds questions that have no real answers and thus expose the fellow being questioned to be not a real doctor but a sort of witch doctor. But no one—at least no one with a modicum of simple human kindness—resents questions from people who honestly want answers. And now and then someone will ask a really interesting question, like, Do you write in the nude? The answer—not generated by computer—is: I don't think I ever have, but if it works, I'm willing to try it."
—"'Ever Et Raw Meat?' and Other Weird Questions," 1987

"I'm always interested in what my readers think, and I'm aware that many of them want to participate in the story. I don't have a problem with that, just so long as they understand that what they think isn't necessarily going to change what I do. That is, I'm never going to say, I've got this story, here it is. Now here's a poll. How do you think I should end it?"
—*The Paris Review*, Fall 2006

§

FEAR

"People ask what scares me. Everything scares me. Bugs are bad. Bugs are real bad. Sometimes I think about taking a bite into a great big hoagie, you know, and...full of bugs. Imagine that. Isn't that awful?"
—"An Evening with Stephen King at the Billerica," 1983

"Scary things are personal. Clowns have freaked me out ever since I was a kid. To me there's something scary, something sinister about such a figure of happiness and fun. I guess that sometimes what makes a scary thing really scary is when we realize there's something sinister behind a nice face."
—*Writing!*, October 2005

"I think the things that scare me are reading about what's happening to the environment, the destruction of the rain forest. I still wish that I didn't know the statistics about the constant rate at which it's disappearing and what's happening to the atmosphere of the planet as a result."
—Press conference, June 2, 1991

"Deep down inside, most of us are afraid. I can still find fear—in fact, I can find more fear now than I used to. I'm afraid the world will blow itself up. I'm afraid of flying. I'm nervous when I don't know where my kids are and I'm still afraid of what's lurking under the bed."
—*Knave*, 1987

"When I was talking about fears, you know, I was talking about the bogeyman and all those things—those are real fears with me. They're not anything that's ruling my life, but one of the things that really does frighten me is the idea of coming in some night to check on my kids…and finding one of them dead."
—"An Evening with Stephen King at the Billerica," 1983

"The mourning for Elvis Presley is a remarkable thing. It began in mid-August of 1977 and has never really stopped. This may be because his passing constitutes the primal death-trauma for the baby-boomer generations. That ordinary death—a heart attack in the bathroom following a strenuous game of racquetball—signaled not one unpalatable fact to us boomers but a pair of them: If the King of Rock could roll into his 40s, then we could too. And if the King of Rock could die of a heart attack (when—gasp!—he didn't really smoke or drink), we were also eligible. His death was one more punch on our colletive ticket out of childhood, whispering one more of adulthood's unpleasant truths: Yes, you're eligible too. If it can happen to him, it can happen to anybody."
—*Entertainment Weekly*, September 17, 2004

"People aren't really afraid of vampires, what they are afraid of is their own death…or the oil bill. When they are reading and watching my stories, they are not afraid of the oil bill, I'll tell you."
—*Lewiston Daily Sun*, April 2, 1974

"[W]e know that sooner or later we're all going to be eating worms, whether it's fifty years or sixty. It might be tomorrow. It might happen today."
—*High Times*, January 1981

"For a long time, death has been one of the great unmentionables in our society, along with sex and how much money you make. It's generally something you try to keep from the kids."
—Speech in Truth or Consequences, New Mexico,
November 19, 1983

"I think people are scared. They're scared of a lot of things: war, poverty, inflation, deflation, deficit, arms race, whatever. And what you do when you've got a lot of things that you're really afraid of is you sublimate them into something that's not real or you find a place to escape—escape pure and simple. So you're

talking about translating the real fears into symbolic fears so that you can deal with them in another way."
—*Miami Herald*, March 25, 1984

"I think that whenever we read a horror story, whether it's about vampires or ghosts, or cars—like in *Christine*, cars that run by themselves—it's telling us all this stuff that we don't believe in one ear, in a very loud voice, but in the other ear, in a very quiet voice, it's whispering about things we really are afraid of. That's why I tell people that I think a lot of the horror movies of the last three or four years are riddled—no pun intended—with cancer; the alien, the thing, the chestburster, the thing that incubates inside this guy is a tumor image; the same thing is true of John Carpenter's remake of *The Thing*—it's more like John Campbell's original story, but informed with our present interests and things like that; it's full of this kind of cancer imagery that has to do with our bodies in revolt. The same thing is true of the Cronenberg films where there are parasites inside, like kind of sexual cancer or in *Scanners* where the guy's head explodes—pretty vivid tumor image."
—*Den of Geek!*, May 13, 1983

"I don't think there's anything that I'm not afraid of, on some level. But if you mean, What are we afraid of, as humans? Chaos. The outsider. We're afraid of change. We're afraid of disruption, and that is what I'm interested in. I mean, there are a lot of people whose writing I really love—one of them is the American poet Philip Booth—who write about ordinary life straight up, but I just can't do that."
—*The Paris Review*, Fall 2006

"When you've got a lot of free-floating anxieties, the horror story or movie helps to sort of conceptualize them, shrink them down to size, make them concrete so they're manipulable. When you can do that, and then it's over at the end and it just sort of blows away, there's probably some minor catharsis involved."
—*Penthouse*, April 1982

"May I be blunt? This fear is that the violence isn't ending but only beginning. It isn't completely rational, but I think I also understand that irrational fears are often the most powerful of all. In this case, the unstated idea is that we have lived well while most of the world lives badly, eaten well while too much of the world goes hungry or actually starves, dressed our children in the best, much of it made by children in other countries who have little but their dreams, many of which are the violent American dreams they see on TV. We have had all this, some of us—maybe a lot of us—seem to think, and there must be a price. There must be a payment. Perhaps there must even be a judgment."

—VEMA keynote address, May 26, 1999

§

FILM ADAPTATIONS
OF HIS WORK

"[When they make a film of your novel] it's like sending a kid off to college. You hope they're going to do well, you hope they're not going to get into trouble, you hope they're going to graduate summa cum laude, you hope they're not going to get hooked on drugs or get into any kind of trouble—but you realize at the same time, this really isn't yours anymore. It's going to belong to someone else."
—*Larry King Live*, April 10, 1986

"[A writer is like] a father who sends his daughter off to college. You hope that the girl is not going to get gang banged at a fraternity, and you hope that the girl is not going to turn into a little roundheels but at the same time, if you've got any intelligence, you realize that at a certain point she has to go her own way and her virginity—her propriety or whatever—is no longer your personal concern. And in the same way, if somebody pays a lot of money for the rights to a book that I wrote and they're going to make a film out of it—I hope that it will be treated well."
—*Twilight Zone*, December 1985

"What it comes down to is, you have to take a 'worst case' attitude—if they screw this up, how am I going to feel? I talked that over with myself, and what I came up with was: I don't care if they destroy it, if they make a terrible movie out of this book, because they can't destroy the book."
—*Twilight Zone*, April 1981

"You have to start with the idea that things are going to change if you let it out of your own back yard. My point of view is that the books are long-distance runners, and they're there long after the films are forgotten."
—*The Philadelphia Inquirer*, April 2, 1994

"Whenever anybody points to the movie and says how bad they are compared to the book, I answer, 'But look how bad it could have been.'"
—*Nashville Tennesseean*, May 5, 1980

"Ultimately, they can't mutilate anything that I wrote because the writing will stand on its own, one way or another."
—*Cinefantastique*, Winter 1978

"As far as film versions of my work goes, the only thing I've tried to insist on with the major works is to try and get as much money as possible. Because if they're going to make them—my idea of the trade-off is, 'Go ahead, make the picture, give me a lot of money and I'll stay out of your face.' Because the books exist in their own life."
—*Prevue*, May-July 1986

"My view has always been that movies are not books and books are not movies. And I don't understand writers who get all wound up in the film adaptations of their novels, as though somehow the novel could be tainted, the novel itself could be tainted by a bad adaptation."
—*Fangoria*, August 1986

"[S]ome interviewer was talking to James Cain, who did *The Postman Always Rings Twice* and all that stuff, and this interviewer was moaning about how the movies had ruined Cain's work and Cain looks around at the books on the shelf behind him and says, 'No, they look just the same to me.' It doesn't hurt the book if they do a terrible movie."
—*Starburst*, 1983

"[I]n my case, more of the movies than not—if we except things like *Return to 'Salem's Lot*, *Children of the Corn 4*, *The Children of the Corn Meet the Leprechaun* or whatever it is—if you do that, then most times you're going to have something that's interesting anyway. That doesn't mean you're not going to

have the occasional thing that's just a train wreck like *Dreamcatcher*, because that happens, right?"
—*Time*, November 23, 2007

"I've liked most of the pictures. I don't go as an active participant unless I wrote the screenplay or something. I go as a moviegoer. It's always kind of fun when it's good, and there are times when it's so close to what I'd imagined, it's like getting a chance to turn my eyeballs around and look inside my own mind and see how things are furnished there."
—*Orange Coast Magazine*, November 1986

"Let's get one thing up front—I like most of the adaptations pretty well. The only two real exceptions to that are *The Shining* and *Children of the Corn*."
—*Fangoria*, August 1986

"Sometimes it's good. Sometimes it's *Children of the Corn*."
—*The Vancouver Sun*, November 22, 2007

"Back in the days of the silents, they made a picture out of A.A. Merritt's *Seven Footprints to Satan* and it's written in one of Forry Ackerman's books that when Merritt saw it he wept. And that would be a standard reaction, I think, among most writers of fantasy whose books have been adapted for the films."
—"Probabilities," September 8, 1979

"They just see it as a loaf of bread or a turkey to be carved up—and that's often just what comes out, too—a turkey."
—*Take One*, January 1979

"You know what John Updike used to say about it: It's the best of all possible worlds when they pay you a lot of money and don't make the movie."
—Speech in Pasadena, California, 1982

"I think *Children of the Corn* is probably the worst adaptation. *Firestarter* has about as much flavor as a great big plateful of cafeteria mashed potatoes. *Christine* should work, but doesn't; it's just dead. *The Shining* just really doesn't seem to work for me, because I don't think Stanley Kubrick understood as much about the genre as maybe he thought he did. But I like most of the other ones,

from *Cat's Eye* to *Cujo* to *Carrie* to *Salem's Lot* to *Maximum Overdrive*. What else am I going to think after I spent a year of my life working on it? That it's awful?"
—*Orange Coast Magazine*, November 1986

"In taking your own work and trying to transfer it to that medium, it isn't an anti-creative act, but it isn't creative either. It's just trying to take out everything that you can from your original work in order to fit a mold."
—*Shayol*, Winter 1982

"I've always thought of screenplays as work for idiots. It took me about five days to do *Creepshow*. Screenwriting is like skating on top of a frozen pond in the winter, whereas writing a novel is like swimming—you have to dive in and get wet."
—*Los Angeles Herald*, January 31, 1989

"I like [screenwriting] because it's fast, I like it because it's visual, and I like it because it's work for idiots in the sense that it's all like skating—it's this totally surface phenomenon. I don't like the fact that everybody in the world wants to put a handprint on what you do."
—*Twilight Zone*, December 1985

"To do a script of a novel that you wrote is like sitting on a suitcase that's full of shit and trying to get it on an airplane. It's a stupid business and I won't do it anymore."
—*Interview*, February 1986

"[W]hen you don't get involved, you are in a no-lose situation, when you can say, 'If it's good, that's based on my work.' And if it's bad, you can say, 'I didn't have anything to do with that.'"
—Speech in Pasadena, California, 1982

"Brian De Palma's *Carrie* was terrific. He handled the material deftly and artistically and got a fine performance out of Sissy Spacek. In many ways, the film is far more stylish than my book, which I still think is a gripping read but is impeded by a certain heaviness, a *Sturm and Drang* quality that's absent from the film."
—*Playboy*, June 1983

"I called up [*Carrie* producer Paul] Monash, and I said, 'You know, Travolta is playing the heavy in this picture, and you want him to sing this love song over the credits, to the girl he's dumping pig's blood on?' And he said, 'Well, how about the Bee Gees?' and I said 'No, I really don't think so.'"
—*Take One*, January 1979

"When that hand comes out of the grave in *Carrie* at the end… Man, I thought I was going to shit my pants!"
—*American Film*, June 1986

"The major thing has to do with why audiences turn away from them, or why they have turned away from movies, since *The Shining*, which is the one that really turned off the Stephen King book fans, is because they don't find me in the movie. Whatever writers have isn't so much style as it is soul or something that's between the mind and the prose that they write."
—*Fangoria*, August 1986

"It disturbs me that [in *The Dead Zone*], of all the babies in New Hampshire, it turns out to be Sarah's own baby that Stillson happens to grab. A lot of the plot choices reflect an obsession in Hollywood that everything has to support everything else, like a house of cards."
—*Fangoria*, April 1984

"I like *Dead Zone*. It's one of my favorite films of all time. David Cronenberg can be so cold and crazy, but *Dead Zone* has a really nice human feel."
—*Ottawa Citizen*, March 15, 2003

"From a commercial sense, I thought Taft was crazy to want *Cujo* from the beginning. I think they were sort of hypnotized by the name, by the idea of saying, 'We have a Stephen King novel,' which has become a little bit like saying 'We've got Paul Newman!'"
—*Famous Monsters*, April 1980

"A lot of these people will just boff around at cocktail parties, have a drink or snort up some cocaine off a mirror, and say, 'Well, I've got an option on the new Stephen King…' You know, a lot of them are real sleazebags, and they just don't care! But if you tie them down to a lot of money, you've got more assurance that the movie will be made, because somebody wants to get their money back."
—*Famous Monsters*, April 1980

"What you can spend is about four million dollars because what they're looking for is a exploitation hit that's going to last two weeks. Nobody's looking to make anything quality out of my stuff."
—*Fangoria*, August 1986

"They kept sort of insisting that I add some kind of Vietnam metaphor for [*Children of the Corn*]. You see this is what I mean when you make a movie you get a lot of people in collaboration, someone really fucks up."
—*Fangoria*, August 1986

"Here is another horror movie, and to me the most horrible thing about it is that it was based on one of my stories. Not very closely—just closely enough so the producers could call it *Stephen King's Children of the Corn*, which it really wasn't… I understand this gobbler made money, but so far I haven't seen any of it, and I'm not sure I want to. It might have corn-borers in it."
—*Castle Rock*, September 1985

"*Firestarter* is one of the worst of the bunch, even though in terms of story it's very close to the original. But it's flavorless; it's like cafeteria mashed potatoes."
—*American Film*, June 1986

"[On *Firestarter*:] There were $3 million worth of special effects and another $3 million of Academy Award-winning talent up there on the screen, and none of it was working. Watching that happen was an incredible, unreal, and painful experience."
—*Cinefantastique*, February 1991

"Shit, *Cat's Eye* is a great movie!"
—*Prevue*, May-July 1986

"The extent of my involvement [with *Stand by Me*] was reading the first draft of the script and telling Rob I thought it was wonderful and thinking privately to myself, 'They'll never make this, it's too much like the story.' But they did."
—*Boston Herald*, July 27, 1986

"I think *Shawshank Redemption* and *Stand by Me* are the two best ones probably. And they're also the ones that people seem to love. They're almost like R-rated Hallmark cards in a way, where people go to them, and they come out feeling good."
—*Nightline*, November 15, 2007

"[Frank Darabont] does it really well, though there are other people who have done my work and I've been pleased with the results. But the only person that I can say has come back for seconds and has really done me proud other than Frank would be Rob Reiner, who did *Stand by Me* and then came back and did *Misery*."
—*Time*, November 23, 2007

"They had cast Christopher Reeve [in *The Running Man*], who's right for the part, and they pulled him out, not bankable, and it's going to be Arnold Schwarzenegger. I'm sorry, I just don't believe this guy against society."
—*Fangoria*, August 1986

"[S]ome woman came up to me at the supermarket once and said, 'Oh, I know who you are, and I'm sure you write wonderful stuff, but I don't read that horror stuff, and I don't go to see those movies.' I said, 'Well, did you like *The Shawshank Redemption*?' She said, 'Oh, I loved that movie. Morgan Freeman was so wonderful.' I said, 'Well, I wrote the story that was based on.' And she said, 'No you didn't. No you didn't!'"
—*The Record*, March 23, 2003

"[*The Stand*] is maybe the one thing I've done where I want to get as much creative control over the movie as I can get. If it's gonna get bitched up, I want to do the bitching up. I don't want to let somebody else do it."
—*Cinefantastique*, Summer 1980

"I call it the bladder factor. People squirm at *Saving Private Ryan* because it's two hours and 50 minutes long. The limiting factor is your bladder. The most successful movies that have been made out of my books have been about the shorter books. That's the bladder factor... *Apt Pupil* is from a novella. It's shorter. And I really like it. I think you're going to like it."
—*The Record*, October 30, 1998

"I ordinarily don't comment far in advance on films based on my work, especially TV films, but in the case of *Desperation* I am going to make an exception because my old partner in crime, Mick Garris, has produced an extraordinary piece of work, and the ensemble cast is outstanding. Ron Perlman as Collie Entragian will haunt your dreams."
—StephenKing.com, February 23, 2005

"I don't want to go out and make political statements. I'm a storyteller. But I said before and I'll say again, if you're trying to do your best work, these things are going to come up, they're going to become part of the story, and people are going to ask questions about it. Is *The Mist* a political story? Is *The Mist* a story that has to do with the dangers of entrenched religion, fundamentalist religion? Is *The Mist* a story about Red vs. Blue? I'm not going to answer any of those questions. You go see the movie."
—*The Vancouver Sun*, November 22, 2007

"[I] think that scripts that are adapted are always easier when they are based on shorter works and I think those actually turn out a little bit better. I think that both *The Mist* and *1408* from last year are really good movies and both are based on shorter works. When you get a long book it's kinda like trying to stuff everything into a suitcase and that can be very difficult."
—*Lilja's Library*, February 20, 2008

"I think it's a very terrifying movie, and I use the word hesitantly. *1408* actually tries to get people into an uncertainty center of their brain. It plays with reality in a way that is very uncomfortable. I really liked it."
—*USA Today*, June 21, 2007

"I'm involved to this extent: For the past 10 years, I've had script approval over most of [the films], cast approval, director, all that stuff. The reason why they gave me that is that they understand—particularly at Castle Rock, which is named after the little town in *Stand by Me*—they know that I'm not going to be unreasonable, that I'm not going to tell them they can't do this or that unless it's something that's frankly overboard. I can think of maybe one or two cases where a name came up and I vetoed it."
—*The Record*, March 23, 2003

§

God and Religion

"[T]he whole tenet of Christianity is that you have to take these things on faith. Well, that's fine. If you can reject your intellect enough to have faith, that's fine."

—*Twilight Zone*, April 1981

"I think that myth and imagination are, in fact, nearly interchangeable concepts, and that belief is the wellspring of both. Belief in what? I don't think it matters very much, to tell you the truth. One god or many. Or that a dime can derail a freight-train."

—*Nightmares & Dreamscapes* (Introduction), 1992

"Yeah, I clearly learned my Bible, and I took a lot of what it says to heart enough to be disgusted by the Jim and Tammy Bakers and the Rex Humbards of the world, where it says 'when you pray go inside your closet and shut the door and do it by yourself, don't do it in front of everybody so that everybody will know how religious you are.' ... I'm not a proselytizer, and I hate organized religion. I think it's one of the roots of real evil that's in our world. If you really unmask Satan, you'll probably find that he's wearing a turnaround collar."

—*Amazing Authors Showcase*, 1988

"My wife is a fallen-away Catholic and I'm a fallen-away Methodist. As a result, while we both keep in our hearts a sort of realization of God, the idea that God must be part of a rational world, I must say that our children are much more familiar with Ronald McDonald than they are with, let's say, Jesus or Peter or Paul or any of those people. They can tell you about the Burger King or the Easter Bunny, but some of this other stuff they're not too cool on."

—"An Evening with Stephen King at the Billerica," 1983

"[A]s a feminist Tabby has never been crazy about the Catholics, where the men make the rules (including the God-given directive to always go in bareback) and the women wash the underwear. And while I believe in God I have no use for organized religion."
—*On Writing*, 2000

"I'd say I'm probably more religious now than ever in my life. I don't go to church or anything like that. Organized religion is always the same thing: sooner or later, somebody drives a sword through your heart."
—*Penthouse*, April 1982

"My feelings towards Christianity are neutral—I believe in God, but not necessarily in organized religion...although I will qualify this by saying that, as a kid brought up in the mostly-lukewarm atmosphere of Methodism, I was always fascinated by the trappings and solemnity of Catholicism. Coincidentally (or maybe not) the only girl I was ever serious about in college is a Catholic, and the woman that I married is a Catholic—of the lapsed variety."
—*Cinefantastique*, Winter 1978

"If there is [a God], it's mysterious and powerful and awesome to even consider the concept, and you have to take it seriously. I understand where Bill Maher is coming from when he says, basically, the world is destroying itself over a bunch of fairy tales about talking snakes and men who are alive inside fishes. I'm very sympathetic to it, but at the same time, given the cosmos that we're living in, it's very persuasive, the idea that there is some kind of first cause that's running things. It might not be the god of Jerry Jenkins and Tim LaHaye, it might not be the god of al-Qaida, and it might not be the god of Abraham, but something very well could be running things. The order of the universe as we see it, the interlocking nature, and the way things work together, are persuasive of the idea that there may be some overarching first cause."
—*Salon*, October 23, 2008

"I don't have too many problems with Roman Catholics who want to go to mass and do their thing and all that. I don't personally like it, and I want to disassociate myself from it. We've got millions of churchgoers in this country who, by their attendance, are giving their stamp of approval to the church which recognized the Inquisition and is, whether intentionally or not, the balance wheel of so much misery over the entire world, from Northern Ireland to wherever."
—*Famous Monsters*, April 1980

"If televangelists are more worried about getting into heaven than they are about life here on earth, why are they always asking viewers for money? And why do so many of them wear sharp suits? Do they think there's going to be a dress code in heaven?"
—*Entertainment Weekly*, January 13, 2006

"I was raised Christian, and I was raised to believe in the idea of the Antichrist. My wife said that—she was raised a Catholic—the attitude of the Catholic church is, give them to me when they're young, and they'll be mine forever. It isn't really true. A lot of us grow up and we grow out of the literal interpretation that we get when we're children, but we bear the scars all our life. Whether they're scars of beauty or scars of ugliness, it's pretty much in the eye of the beholder."
—*Salon*, October 23, 2008

"Churches make morals, which, I suppose, is useful... So is Tupperware, in its way."
—*Cinefantastique*, Winter 1978

"I don't see myself as God's stenographer. [I'm] someone who believes in God, believes that God is a logical outgrowth of the fact that life fits together as well as it does, but that doesn't mean that we know God's mind. That's not to say that the idea of religion is a good thing, because we can see that it's a bad thing."
—*The World of Fandom*, 1996

"I was interested in *The Passion* [*of the Christ*] phenomenon. ... For one thing, I wanted to find out if Christians eat popcorn with their crucifixion (turns out they do, usually in the big tubs). In some ways, you could tell this was no ordinary afternoon crowd; there was a fair selection of Christian wear (my favorite T shirt read JESUS IS THE BIG ONE), and absolutely nobody was giving anyone else hell for cutting the refreshment line. These are people who take hell seriously."
—*Entertainment Weekly*, March 19, 2004

"My generation traded God for Martha Stewart. She's this priestess of etiquette who says that when you shovel snow from your drive, you oughta leave an inch or two at the sides, because it looks so nice."
—*The Observer*, August 9, 1998

"As to what I think about God: I think that He's out there. A more important question is what God thinks about me."
—Lecture at Virginia Beach, September 22, 1986

"I think that probably there is an afterlife, but it's probably a physiological phenomenon that occurs at the moment of death. You know how if you're doing something that you really like how fast the time goes by? And if you're doing something you really hate how it—did you ever read *Catch-22*? You remember the guy who tried to be bored because he said he'd live longer—his name was Milo Mindbender? Well, I think that when we die, a chemical may be released that creates a feeling of great euphoria and that so-called white light that people talk about in the death experience, and that what follows is some sort of hallucination that occurs in instants at the time of dying but may seem, indeed, like it goes on for eternity, and that you get what you believe you will get. That is to say, if you thought you were going to go to heaven, that you were a good person, you'll go, but if you're guilt-ridden and thought you were going to hell, you will go to hell, but it will be a hell of your own making."
—*Amazing Authors Showcase*, 1988

"[On *Desperation*:] There's been a lot of criticism of the book where they say the God stuff really turns them off. I'm thinking to myself that these guys have no problems with vampires, demons, golems, werewolves, and you name it. If you try to bring in a God who can take sardines and crackers and turn it into loaves and fishes, then these people have a problem. I say to myself, if you have a real problem then I'm doing what a novel of suspense and horror is supposed to do, which is to just scratch below the surface and sort of rub your nerves the wrong way."
—*The World of Fandom*, 1996

"I am a religious man. Well, I'm a spiritual man. I certainly believe in God, and I meditate on a regular basis, and try to stay in touch with the God of my understanding. But I haven't been through the doors of the church, I don't think since my mother-in-law died. And I certainly don't have anything against churches per se. I'm not a vampire type, when somebody shows me the cross or something like that. But organized religion gives me the creeps."
—*Nightline*, November 15, 2007

§

HIMSELF

"They say 'Are you really a scary guy?' And I say, 'Sure, I've got the heart of a small boy... I keep it in a jar on my desk.' And that keeps them away."
—*Amazon Fishbowl with Bill Maher*, 2006

"Most of [my books] have been plain fiction for plain folks, the literary equivalent of a Big Mac and large fries from McDonald's. I am able to recognize elegant prose and to respond to it, but have found it difficult or imposing to write it myself."
—*Different Seasons* (Afterword), 1982

"I've heard people say, 'Oh, God, Stephen King! He writes like Dickens!' Well, bullshit. Nobody writes like Dickens. Nobody ever did, and nobody ever will."
—*Nightline*, November 15, 2007

"If I'm alive in twenty years, I suppose I'll still be writing things, unless I go dry, which I guess is always a possibility. If that happened I'd like to be able to accept it with grace and not stick a gun in my mouth the way that Hemingway did."
—"An Evening with Stephen King at the Billerica," 1983

"I'll die. Or I'll get Alzheimer's disease or something. You see, I'm a horror writer; I can think of all sorts of nasty reasons to stop [writing]. I thought that I would be done after *The Dark Tower* books. But you don't get to say 'when' in a business like this. Ideas surface and say, 'Write me!' So here I am, at the same old stand."
—*Writing!*, October 2005

"I'd say that what I do is like a crack in the mirror. If you go back over the books from *Carrie* on up, what you see is an observation of ordinary middle-class American life as it's lived at the time that particular book was written. In every life you get to a point where you have to deal with something that's inexplicable to you, whether it's the doctor saying you have cancer or a prank phone call. So whether you talk about ghosts or vampires or Nazi war criminals living down the block, we're still talking about the same thing, which is an intrusion of the extraordinary into ordinary life and how we deal with it. What that shows about our character and our interactions with others and the society we live in interests me a lot more than monsters and vampires and ghouls and ghosts."
      —*The Paris Review*, Fall 2006

"I also employed the world-famous Hemingway Defense. Although never clearly articulated (it would not be manly to do so), the Hemingway Defense goes something like this: as a writer, I am a very sensitive fellow, but I am also a man, and real men don't give into their sensitivities. Only sissy-men do that. Therefore I drink. How else can I face the existential horror of it all and continue to work?"
      —*On Writing*, 2000

"I like to feel that I give an honest deal for the dollar or pound. I mean shit, these guys are selling at $18.95 and I don't want anybody to go get that book and say, 'Well, I got about $13.50 out of this, I want my change.' What you'd like to hear is for some guy to go pay $18.95 for *Christine* and say, 'Gee, I got $19.50's worth."
      —*Sounds*, May 21, 1983

"I don't think I could've gotten a hardcover house in hell to look at my stuff if it hadn't been for *The Exorcist* and some of those others."
      —*Fangoria*, April 1984

"Sure, I'm a commercial writer. I'd like to get filthy rich and own a yacht. But I write only to please myself, and to entertain myself. For me, my books are home movies."
      —*Cinefantastique*, Winter 1978

"I am a writer by trade, which means that the most interesting things that have happened to me have happened in my dreams."
      —*Danse Macabre*, 1981

"Writing books is the only thing I know how to do really. I'm like Paul, the hero in *Misery*, in that way. I lead a fairly boring life, except when I write. And when I write, man, I have wonderful adventures."
—"Turning the Thumbscrews on the Reader," 1987

"I hate to tour and I hate interviews. Not because you meet people that are bad people. You don't. But basically I'm a fairly boring person. There's only so many stories I can tell about myself. I don't live life in the fast lane, and I'm not very interested in advertising myself."
—*Orange Coast Magazine*, November 1986

"All the elements of storytelling have their part to play, but for me the most important thing is that I want the readers to turn the page. I want to make a connection with them that's emotional. I want to make them sweat a little, laugh a little, and even cry."
—*Read*, October 21, 2005

"I think this bravery in the face of horror is one of the things that people respond to in my work. I don't think that people just want to see a kind of supernatural car crash."
—*Houston Chronicle*, September 30, 1979

"I like to scare people, and people like to be scared. That's all there is to it."
—*Twilight Zone*, April 1981

"I want to scare the shit out of you if I can. That's what I'm there to do. I like to go for the jugular."
—*Twilight Zone*, April 1981

"One of my jobs is to assault your emotions—to come and get you—and I'll use the tools that come to hand. It may be to scare the hell out of you but it may also be to get you in a more subversive way, you know, to make you feel sad. If I can make you sad, that's good. If I can make you laugh, that's good."
—*The Times*, October 21, 2006

"I will take you way past the stop sign, I will take you beyond the things you think that you want to know about, right down into the very depths. I will touch your darkest phobias. You may think you want to know, but by the time you realize you don't—well, sorry buddy, but it's just too damned late..."
—*Knave*, 1987

"I'm not afraid of spiraling down into a very unpleasant conclusion. Partly because I think life sometimes does that, and also because I was really impressed by the American naturalists and the British naturalists... They all seem to say the same thing: Things are not ever going to get any better, and if you want to see how things go, just think about what's going to happen to you."
—Bibliographic information unknown

"When I speak in public—a thing I do as rarely as possible—I usually don't speak from a prepared text and I hardly ever try to say anything serious; to misquote Mark Twain, I feel that anyone looking for a moral should be hung and anyone looking for a plot should be shot."
—VEMA keynote address, May 26, 1999

"If I were a Henry James or Jane Austen sort of guy, writing only about toffs or smart college folks, I'd hardly ever have to use a dirty word or a profane phrase; I might never have had a book banned from America's school libraries or gotten a letter from some helpful fundamentalist fellow who wants me to know that I'm going to burn in hell, where all my millions of dollars won't buy me so much as a single drink of water. I did not, however, grow up among folks of that sort. I grew up as a part of America's lower middle class, and they're the people I can write about with the most honesty and knowledge. It means that they say shit more often than sugar when they bang their thumbs."
—*On Writing*, 2000

"I write about 'what if'... Literary writers, the highbrows, say 'what next?' I'm not interested in that. I'm a 'what if' writer."
—*Toronto Star*, October 5, 1983

"[Joyce Carol Oates] gets a lot of ink because she's a very good writer, a classy writer. And I get a lot of ink because I make a lot of money. I'm a salami writer. I try to write good salami, but salami is salami. You can't sell it as caviar. Updike I'm not, thank God."
—*West Magazine*, July 19, 1987

"*Carrie* dealt with telekinesis. But I have never tried to write hardcore science fiction. I got Cs and Bs in biology and chemistry."
—*Milwaukee Journal*, September 15, 1980

"I've never really had any goals other than to tell stories and to try and keep things fresh. So I guess I'm always setting the goal a step ahead. I'm having fun; is that a goal?"
—AOL chat, October 10, 2000

"The fact is, almost all of the stuff I have written—and that includes a lot of the funny stuff—was written in a serious frame of mind… I do what I do for the most serious reasons: love, money, and obsession."
—*Four Past Midnight* (Note on The Sun Dog), 1990

"[Y]ou get pigeonholed after a while. You are a horror writer. You become that person. It's like that American Express ad I did, where they put you in an old dark house, you know, so that you become almost like a brand name yourself. But it doesn't have anything to do with who you are. That's not a real person— that persona, or that thing. For instance, if I do an autographing, I always feel disappointed going in, because I feel like I can't do what they want me to do. I can't come in in a sweeping black cloak and then suddenly disappear at the end of it."
—*Larry King Live*, April 10, 1986

"We love our categories neat and clean in America; if you think it over, you almost have to agree that it's guns, cheeseburgers, and categories that made this country great (okay, you can throw in the Louisiana Purchase, if you're of a geographical bent). I realized years ago that I had been categorized as the Horror Guy. Had to happen. Alfred Hitchcock and Rod Serling were both dead, and Hitchcock was British, anyway."
—*Entertainment Weekly*, August 4, 2006

"I think the world needs Santa Claus…and America really needs Ronald McDonald. But America also needs a boogeyman. And Alfred Hitchcock's dead, so I got the job."
—*Writing!*, October 2005

"Halloween has been my least favorite holiday ever since the mid-'80s, when trick-or-treaters started showing up at my house in battalions, many dressed as Pennywise the Clown. That was when I realized I'd been elected America's Guru of Grue without even running for the position."
—*Entertainment Weekly*, October 28, 2005

"At some point between *Salem's Lot*, my second book, and *The Dead Zone*, my sixth, I became America's Best-Loved Boogeyman."
—*Entertainment Weekly*, August 2, 1991

"A lot of the books I've written are about ordinary American life. And by using the elements I do, people have slapped this label on me and they say, 'Well, he's a horror writer.' It's terrific, it's wonderful. It has made it possible to send my kids to school and the mortgages are paid off, you know. So I don't have a problem with it."
—*The Times*, October 21, 2006

"I don't think I ever will be taken seriously. People write to me and say how much they enjoy my books, but when someone walks by with a book by John Barth in their hands, they hide me so they won't get caught."
—*Detroit Free Press*, November 12, 1982

"The bottom line is always sales and these guys [Tom Clancy and Danielle Steel] outsell me, Grisham outsells me four to one. It's not a big deal to me anymore. … Do I really want to bust my ass to be on [*The New York Times* bestseller list] along with Danielle Steel and David Baldacci and the born-again books?"
—*Pittsburgh Post-Gazette*, October 31, 2006

"A lot of writers, they die and their books are gone. It could well happen to me. If anything would help me stay around, it's horror. It's the strontium 90 of literature. It has a hell of a half-life."
—*The Record*, October 30, 1998

"The real test of how good a writer is, particularly a popular writer, is whether or not their work can outlast their deaths by five, ten, fifteen years. That remains to be seen, but I think a lot of this stuff will be in the libraries and 50 years from now or 100 years from now. After I'm dead some eleven year old kid will be going along through the racks the way I went through the library stacks and discovered Richard Matheson and Algernon Blackwood, and he'll find this dusty book and he'll take it home and he'll lose an afternoon."

—*Miami Herald*, March 25, 1984

"I'd just like to be remembered. 'Cause I got a piece about some writer whose name I think was Joseph Hergeshimer or something like that, who was a big bestseller around the beginning of the 20th Century. And I'd never heard of him."

—*Inside*, April 4, 1986

"You never know who's going to be popular in fifty years. Who is going to be in, in a literary sense, and who's not. If I had to predict which of my books people will pick up a hundred years from now, if they pick up any, I'd begin with *The Stand* and *The Shining*. And *Salem's Lot*—because people like vampire stories, and its premise is the classic vampire story. It doesn't have any particular bells or whistles. It's not fancy, it's just scary. So I think people will pick that up for a while."

—*The Paris Review*, Fall 2006

"If I had to guess, I'd say that I'll be sort of the Somerset Maugham of horror. At the time of his greatest popularity, he was very popular and there had been dozens and dozens of movies made from his books. But now nobody really knows who he is."

—*Nightline*, November 15, 2007

"A writer has only a finite number of stories to write. I think I'm very near the end of publishing my work... I don't want to descend into self-parody. I've written most of the things people are going to appreciate. After this, it might just be the blabberings of a tiresome old uncle. I don't want to become Harold Robbins."

—*The Gazette*, September 20, 1998

"I have never felt like I was creating anything. For me, writing is like walking through a desert and all at once, poking up through the hardpan, I see the top of a chimney. I know there's a house there, and I'm pretty sure I can dig it up if I want. That's how I feel. It's like the stories are already there. What they pay me for is the leap of faith that says: 'If I sit down and do this, everything will come out okay."

—*Read*, October 21, 2005

"I've had about three original ideas in my life. The rest of them were bounces. I sense the limitations of where my talents are."
—*Time*, October 6, 1986

"I've written more than once about the joy of writing and see no need to reheat that particular skillet of hash at this late date, but here's a confession: I also take an amateur's slightly crazed pleasure in the business side of what I do. I like to goof widdit, do a little media cross-pollination and envelope-pushing. I've tried doing visual novels (*Storm of the Century*, *Rose Red*), serial novels (*The Green Mile*), and serial novels on the Internet (*The Plant*). It's not about making more money or even precisely about creating new markets; it's about trying to see the act, art, and craft of writing in different ways, thereby refreshing the process and keeping the resulting artifacts—the stories, in other words—as bright as possible."
—*Everything's Eventual* (Introduction), 2001

"You see, I am my work to a large extent. Work takes most of the energy. It's what gives me pleasure. It is the toy."
—*Parents Magazine*, January 1982

"I'd like to think that I have gotten better, that the writer you're talking to now is a better craftsman than the one who wrote *Carrie* when he was 22 or 23 years old. But I don't detect in my own work any particular late blossoming."
—*Time*, April 1, 2002

"For the record, this story about me retiring came out of *The Los Angeles Times*. I did an interview with them where I said 'I'm pretty well wrapped up, I don't know if I have a lot else to say, and I don't want to repeat myself.' And they jumped from that to 'Stephen King is retiring.' I don't even bother to talk about it anymore, because people get the idea in their mind and they're going to believe it."
—*The Record*, March 23, 2003

"[On turning 60:] I look the same as I ever did when I look in the mirror. I can still see the kid there. But people seeing you see someone who's older. I went to a movie theater, and the woman asked if I wanted my golden-ager discount. I asked how old you have to be for that, and she said 65. I said 'Not yet, dear.'"
—*The Berkshire Eagle*, January 21, 2008

"I do two different kinds of books. I think of books like *The Stand, Desperation,* and the *Dark Tower* series as books that go out. Then there are books like *Pet Sematary, Misery, The Shining,* and *Dolores Claiborne* that go in. Fans usually will either like the outies or they'll like the innies. But they won't like both."
—*The Paris Review,* Fall 2006

§

HIS BOOKS

"I started *Carrie* as a short story, but then it crossed my mind that there ought to be a longer fuse before the explosion and the next thing I knew it had grown into a novel."

—*Milwaukee Journal*, September 15, 1980

"[On *Carrie*:] You don't write a novel that could be subtitled 'High School Confidential' without the thought foremost in your mind that there is a junk, kitschy side of America that's very compelling and that's fun to play with."

—*Take One*, January 1979

"[On *Salem's Lot*:] We got sitting around and rapping at the dinner table about what would happen if Dracula came back today, in modern dress. And my first reaction was that he'd go to New York and get run over by a taxicab! But that question wouldn't go away; it kept coming back when I was bored or just sitting around."

—*Famous Monsters*, April 1980

"*Salem's Lot* had been read at NAL with a great deal of enthusiasm, much of it undoubtedly because they recognized a brand name potential beginning to shape up. Horror was big in those days…and I showed no signs with my second book of exchanging my fright wig and Lon Chaney makeup for a pipe and tweed jacket and writing something Deep and Meaningful."

—*Fear Itself*, 1982

"There will always be a special cold place in my heart for *Salem's Lot*. It seemed to capture some of the special things about living in a small town that I'd known all my life. It's funny, but after reading the book people will say to me, 'You must really hate Maine.' And I really like it here. The novel shows a lot of scars about the town. But so much of it is a love song to growing up in a small town."
—*Yankee*, March 1979

"In a way, *The Shining* is sort of like I Love Lucy gone bad. In a resort hotel—[adopts a Desi Arnaz accent] 'Loo-cee, I'm home!'"
—*Larry King Live*, April 10, 1986

"If there's anything that I regret in my career, it's publishing the novel *Rage*. It's a story about a kid who's very severely disturbed and brings a gun to school, kills his teacher, and holds his class hostage over the course of the day. My view when this comes up is that most people who commit crimes of that nature are already so disturbed; that if they didn't do it one way, they would do it another way. It was evil."
—*60 Minutes*, February 16, 1997

"Do I think that *Rage* may have provoked [high school shooter Michael] Carneal, or any other badly-adjusted young person, to resort to the gun? It's an important question, because it goes to the very heart of the wrangle over who's to blame. You might as well ask if I believe that the mere presence of a gun makes some people want to use that gun. The answer is troubling, but it needs to be faced: in some cases, yes. Probably it does. Often? No, I don't believe so. How often is too often? That's not for me or any other single person to say. It's a question each part of our society must answer for itself, as each state, for instance, must answer the question of when a kid is old enough to have a driver's license or buy a drink."
—VEMA keynote address, May 26, 1999

"I think that the actual impetus to write *The Stand* came from a chemical-biological spill in Utah. This stuff got loose that was like Agent Orange, except more deadly, and it killed a bunch of sheep because the wind happened to be blowing away from Salt Lake City and into the barrens."
—"An Evening with Stephen King at the Billerica," 1983

"*The Stand* was particularly fulfilling, because I got a chance to scrub the whole human race and, man, it was fun! Sitting at the typewriter, I felt just like Alexander lifting his sword over the Gordian knot and snarling, 'Fuck unraveling it; I'll do it my way!' Much of the compulsive, driven feeling I had while I worked on *The Stand* came from the vicarious thrill of imagining an entire entrenched social order destroyed in one stroke. That's the mad bomber side of my character, I suppose."
—*Playboy*, June 1983

"I had a bad moment when I was working on *The Stand*. I'd been involved with the book for about two years. I felt like my blood was really flowing out of my stomach, and if I didn't finish the book and staunch the flow I'd just die. Then I look in a bookstore and there's this book out called *Survivors* by Terry Nation… It was about a virus decimating the world and the survivors that were left, and I thought, 'Great, this guy has just written my book.'"
—*Famous Monsters*, April 1980

"I sat down to write [*The Dead Zone*], only I went back a little further and began to ask myself all these other questions about what would happen if you could really see the future. The more I wrote, the more it seemed like just a really fucking horrible thing, you know? People wouldn't like you!"
—*Famous Monsters*, April 1980

"The story [of *The Dead Zone*] was supposed to be about this guy who eventually would shake hands with the man who is going to blow up the world. I got interested in the idea of whether it would be possible to write a moral novel where the assassin, an American assassin, actually was a good guy or where the act would be justified."
—*American Film*, June 1986

"[*Firestarter*] came mostly from occasionally reading articles about pyrokinesis, or maybe I should say auto-pyrokinesis, people who just burn up under mysterious circumstances. … I got to playing with the idea of what would happen if somebody had that ability and could control it. I had a lot of fun writing that book!"
—*Famous Monsters*, April 1980

"Charlie McGee, in *Firestarter*, was very consciously patterned on my daughter, because I know how she looks, I know how she walks, I know what makes her mad. I was able to use that, but only to a certain degree. Beyond that, if you tie yourself to your own children, you limit your range. So I took Naomi, used her as the frame, and then went where I wanted."
—*Parents Magazine*, January 1982

"[On *The Running Man* being rejected:] I muttered a few words to my wife—something to the effect that George Orwell and Jonathan Swift had done quite well with negative utopias—and tossed the book in a drawer, where it stayed for eight or nine years."
—*Rotten Rejections*, 1990

"There's a book called *The Running Man*, which ends with a guy crashing a hijacked jetliner into a skyscraper, and that's the first thing I thought of after 9/11, was my God, somebody actually did that."
—*Salon*, October 23, 2008

"[On *Cujo*:] The idea was the mother and son being trapped over a period of time. In fact, the original idea was that she would contract rabies, and the central conflict of the book would be her struggle to keep from hurting her son as she was overwhelmed by madness, which is kind of a repeat of some of what goes on in *The Shining*."
—*Writer's Digest*, March 1992

"[W]hen *Cujo* was done, I thought, 'This is really not very good; people are not going to like it when this little boy dies.' And I like to please people. So I tried to rewrite the ending so the little boy would live, but it was really tinny and false. I said, 'I'm sorry, the kid is dead. He's just dead, that's all.' So that's the way I left it."
—*Amazing Authors Showcase*, 1988

"[O]ne of the reasons I think I've had some problems with *Cujo* is because people get a little bit worried when they read a book about this woman and kid trapped in a car by a Saint Bernard, and they say, 'This could really happen.' Then they write me a letter that says, 'Gee, I liked your vampire novel better,

I liked *The Shining* better, because we know in our hearts that there are no vampires, and we are sure in our hearts that there are no hotels haunted by ghosts that come to life."
  —*Penthouse*, April 1982

"Except for the prison break story, they're all sort of horror stories [in *Different Seasons*]. The worst one isn't the supernatural one; I think it's *Apt Pupil* about this old guy and a boy. That's a dreadful story. Unghh! Nasty."
  —*Shayol*, Winter 1982

"My characters become very real to me. I wrote a series of books called *The Dark Tower*, and I lived with those characters from the age of about 22 up until when I finished the last one when I was 56. That's like 34 years all told. I'd been doing some of those characters longer than I've been with my children. Some of them had to die and that was tough. Anybody will tell you that imaginary friends are as real as real people sometimes. Lucky for me, I still know the difference or else they'd put me away in a room."
  —*Writing!*, October 2005

"There's a novel coming out called *Christine* in May. It's a great big long book and it's the first horror novel I've done, I think, since *The Shining*. I think I've only done two: *Salem's Lot* and *The Shining* and now *Christine* is a real horror novel. That's all I'm going to say about it. Except it's scary. It's fun, too."
  —*Shayol*, Winter 1982

"I don't know how Chrysler feels about *Christine*, any more than I know how the Ford Company feels about *Cujo* in which a woman is stranded in a Pinto. But they should feel happy, because it's a pretty lively car and it lasts a long time. It's like a Timex watch—it takes a licking and goes on ticking."
  —*Twilight Zone*, February 1984

"[On *Christine*:] It was like *Happy Days* gone mad."
  —Lecture at Virginia Beach, September 22, 1986

"I wish that [*Cycle of the Werewolf*] could have either been more or less, in terms of the book project, because it sorta got out of hand there. It seems thin to me, for the price."
  —*Fangoria*, April 1984

"[*Pet Sematary* is] supposed to be a reflection on what happens when people in a materialistic society, people who live only for materialistic reasons, come into contact with questions of faith and death and outside forces."
—*American Film*, June 1986

"There's a little girl in *Pet Sematary* who lives. Nobody else lives. And there's no rhyme or reason for it. There'd be more justification in that story—in the sense of a final tying up of loose ends—if she died, too. But that isn't the way life is."
—*Fangoria*, April 1984

"With The *Eyes of the Dragon*, I made a conscious decision that it was going to be a book that would be cast more in the mold of the stuff that my daughter likes. She likes books about the horse clans and about wizards and magic."
—*WB #145*, 1987

"I thought it would be a good one to go out with. Called *It*. I should call it *Shit*."
—*Penthouse*, April 1982

"Sometime in the summer of 1981 I realized that I had to write about the troll under the bridge or leave him—*It*—forever. Part of me cried to let it go. But part of me cried for the chance; did more than cry: it demanded. I remember sitting on the porch, smoking, asking myself if I had really gotten old enough to be afraid to try, to just jump in and drive fast."
—"How It Happened," 1986

"From inception to conclusion, *It* took seven years to write. I did other things in that time: wrote a novel (*Pet Sematary*), collaborated on another with my friend Peter Straub (*The Talisman*), wrote three novels that aren't yet published, nine short stories, six novellas, and three screenplays (and directed one of them). But Derry never escaped my mind..."
—"How It Happened," 1986

"I have scared myself on three occasions, and one of them is in the book I just read to you [*Misery*] where something extremely nasty happens later, and I just passed that point in the rewrite and realized to myself that I've been dragging my feet because I knew when I got up there to the axe and the blowtorch, things were going to be nasty and I didn't want to write that."
—Lecture at Virginia Beach, September 22, 1986

"I got done with *Misery* and I could hardly believe what I'd done. I'd written a book that consisted of two characters in one room. In some ways, I worked harder on that book than on anything before. It's not like anything I ever wrote. In a lot of my other books there are characters who are writers, but the books are not about writing; *Misery* is."

—"Turning the Thumbscrews on the Reader," 1987

"[*The Tommyknockers* is] science fiction of a type. But the people who write science fiction are going to look down their noses and say, 'This is crap, because it doesn't say how anything works.'"

—*WB* #145, 1987

"With *Gerald's Game*, it was like an unplanned pregnancy... I had a dream with something salvageable in it, and I said: 'Oh, that's wonderful, what a great idea.' I wanted to start writing it, not because I had a whole story but because it was one of these situations that's so interesting you figure if you start on it, things will suggest themselves."

—*Writing!*, October 2005

"*Gerald's Game* started with the concept of the woman being chained to the bed. I'd written a book before, where a woman and a small child were stuck in a car that was sort of surrounded, if you will, by a rabid Saint Bernard. That book was called *Cujo*. And essentially, what a lot of that book was, was two people in a very small room, although it did have a shifting perspective so that it went to other characters. And I thought, originally, this was the takeoff point for the book: wouldn't it be interesting to see what would happen if you had one character in a room?"

—"Fresh Air," July 2, 2010

"[On *Desperation*:] It seemed to me that most people who are writing novels of supernatural suspense are very interested in evil, and the evil side resonates for them. And I wanted to see if I could create a strong force of good and desperation, as well. So it's a very Christian novel in that way, too. It's going to make some people uncomfortable, I think."

—*Christianity Today*, March 6, 2000

"I used to have these activity books that I played with on rainy days when I was a kid. They had this trick where you could get an interesting look at your face, a different look of your face, by placing the mirror perpendicular to half of your

face. It makes a reflection that is a whole face. In a way, that is what *The Regula-tors* and *Desperation* are."
—*The World of Fandom*, 1996

"[On *Bag of Bones*:] I think that people sense it's a real novel in a way that some of my novels are not. I set out to make it a Gothic, but I wasn't consciously writing a departure from other things. Nobody sets out to write a departure. If they do, they totally screw it up. What you do is what turns your dials, what juices you up. The bowlers say, 'If you work the spares, the strikes will take care of themselves.'"
—*The Record*, October 30, 1998

"I hope *Bag of Bones* gave you at least one sleepless night. Sorry 'bout that; it's just the way I am. It gave me one or two, and ever since writing it I'm nervous about going down into the cellar—part of me keeps expecting the door to slam, the light to go out, and the knocking to start. But for me, at least, that's part of the fun. If that makes me sick, hey, don't call the doctor."
—Letter to reviewers of *Hearts in Atlantis*, May 1999

"*Wizard and Glass* is finally done. It's a long book, and the manuscript I turned in was 1,500 pages long. I think it's good and I know it's overdue. I've been getting more and more mail from pissed off fans saying, 'You know, these people have been on this friggin' train for about five years now. You ever going to finish this story?' The worst one was from this lady who said she really loved the stories, a grandmother of seventy-three with Parkinson's disease, and she had this fear that she was going to die before I finished the story. She was hoping I'd write one more before I she got to feeble to read them."
—*Worlds of Fandom*, 1996

"I've never tried to write a young adult book. But if there was such a thing as a Stephen King young adult novel, it would be *The Girl Who Loved Tom Gordon*."
—*Writing!*, October 2005

"[*Dreamcatcher*] was written by a very sick man. It comes by that feverishness honestly. There were periods every day when I couldn't have written to save my life, and there were periods of the day when I was relatively pain-free, but I was stoned on painkillers."
—*Ottawa Citizen*, March 15, 2003

"Sometimes I'll use film [as inspiration]. In *Wolves of the Calla*, one of the seven books in the *Dark Tower* series, I decided to see if I couldn't retell *Seven Samurai*, that Kurosawa film, and *The Magnificent Seven*. The story is the same, of course, in both cases. It's about these farmers who hire gunslingers to defend their town against bandits, who keep coming to steal their crops. But I wanted to up the ante a little bit. So in my version, instead of crops, the bandits steal children."

—*The Paris Review*, Fall 2006

"My favorite book is *Lisey's Story*, which is why I'm here. [Laughs.] You know, I like *Misery*, and I have a soft spot for *The Dead Zone* because I thought that was my first real novel, but there were a lot of good ones that I still like. And I like *Cujo*, because that was the first one set all in one place."

—Q&A in Portland, Oregon, November 2, 2006

"*Just After Sunset*, it's called. I wanted to call it *Unnatural Acts of Human Intercourse*, and the publisher had a hissy-fit."

—StephenKing.com, September 4, 2008

"Several Internet writers have speculated on a perceived similarity between *Under the Dome* and *The Simpsons Movie*, where, according to Wikipedia, Homer's town of Springfield is isolated inside a large glass dome... I can't speak personally to this, because I have never seen the movie, and the similarity came as a complete surprise to me...although I know, from personal experience, that the similarity will turn out to be casual. Unless there's deliberate copying (sometimes known as 'plagiarism'), stories can no more be alike than snowflakes. The reason is simple: no two human imaginations are exactly alike."

—StephenKing.com, September 15, 2009

"We're all *Under the Dome*. There's limited food and resources and exploding populations, which has led to unpleasant conditions in some parts of the world. I tried to create a tiny scale model of where we all are."

—*Bangor Daily News*, November 9, 2009

§

Hollywood
and the Movies

"I remember going to the Drive-In and seeing *Creature from the Black Lagoon*. … And I said, 'I wanna do that! I'm really scared. I want to make people as scared as I am.'"
　　　　　—"Probabilities," September 8, 1979

"*Night of the Living Dead* has been around so long that it's become the cinematic equivalent of a knock-knock joke, but I still remember the pure horror I felt the first time I saw the little girl stabbing her mother to death with a garden trowel. What I remember thinking as I watched those crazy shadows bounce around at the whim of a swinging lightbulb on the end of an electrical cord is 'I'm in the hands of a lunatic, and he will stop at nothing to scare me.' I've never in my life been more frightened in a movie theater."
　　　　　—*Entertainment Weekly*, November 5, 2003

"People would come to laugh at *Night of the Living Dead*. This was in the old days before it became a 'cult.' And they'd be stunned to silence. About halfway through the film, all the joking would stop and they would be stunned to silence. These college kids who were supposed to be smart asses, they'd be sitting there… I mean, there were girls who were literally being helped out by their boyfriends with their faces deadly white."
　　　　　—*Starburst*, 1983

"I'm case-hardened to horror, but *A Nightmare on Elm Street*, *Friday the 13th*, and *Halloween* all scared the hell out of me (although I believe that *The Texas Chainsaw Massacre*, a film to which there have also been a number of paltry sequels, is still the all-time champeen when it comes to pure fright)."
—*Entertainment Weekly*, August 22, 2003

"I've seen all the *Halloween* movies. In the '80s I even had a button suggesting that Michael Myers and Jamie Lee Curtis would make a hell of a presidential ticket. Do you want to tell me—seriously—that Saddam Hussein would have kept rattling his saber once he started hearing that creepy John Carpenter piano music?"
—*Entertainment Weekly*, August 22, 2003

"[F]ifty years later I can still remember the sense of dismay I felt when Bambi's mother was killed, leaving the poor little feller all alone. I was a single-parent child myself, and I spent many long nights after lights-out thinking about Bambi and wondering what would happen to me if something happened to my mother. I still remember the simple power of the film's most potent line: 'Man was in the forest.'"
—*Entertainment Weekly*, November 5, 2003

"I don't think gore is necessarily bad—it can be used well, as in *Psycho*. There have been some really bad horror movies lately, because they were made by people who don't care about the genre."
—*Footsteps*, November 1986

"Big movies demand big explanations, which are usually tiresome, and big backstories, which are usually cumbersome. If a studio is going to spend $80 or $100 million in hopes of making $300 or $400 million more, they feel a need to shove WHAT IT ALL MEANS down the audience's throat. Is there a serial killer? Then his mommy didn't love him (insert flashback). A monster from outer space? Its planet exploded, of course (and the poor misunderstood thing probably needs a juicy Earth woman to make sexy with). But nightmares exist outside of logic, and there's little fun to be had in explanations; they're antithetical to the poetry of fear."
—*Entertainment Weekly*, July 3, 2008

"When I met Sam Raimi at the Cannes Film Festival in May of 1982, my first thought was that this fellow was one of three things: a busboy, a runaway American high school student, or a genius."
—*Twilight Zone*, November 1982

"Hollywood people are crazy; they're not like us."
—Lecture at Virginia Beach, September 22, 1986

"They buy options, these people, like you or I would buy a loaf of bread, mostly because if it doesn't work out they can take a tax loss."
—*Take One*, January 1979

"A lot of people in Hollywood only see the buck, and they're perfectly willing to take a fine fantasy novel, something by Fritz Leiber or H.P. Lovecraft, and turn it into a piece of drive-in tripe that's gonna play for two weeks and be gone. They don't care, because they only laid out about four hundred thousand dollars on the picture anyway. They make back the negative cost and another million, and everybody goes home happy."
—*Famous Monsters*, April 1980

"Nobody ever sets out to make a bad movie, but sometimes they're just set out to make money and that's just as bad. That's a recipe for disaster."
—*Fangoria*, August 1986

"My idea of a perfect horror film would be one where you'd have to have nurses and doctors on duty with crash wagons because people would have heart attacks. People would crawl out with large wet spots on their trousers. It would be that kind of experience. They'd say, 'What the hell are you doing with me?' The answer: 'What you wanted. We're scaring you."
—*Interview*, 1989

"My experience with Hollywood has always been that the first thing you hear is something like, 'This is the greatest screenplay since *Ben Hur*!' That's followed by 'We want to make a few changes,' and the 'few changes' go on for seven months until they finally drop the project."
—*Cinefantastique*, September-October 1982

"There's nothing wrong with having fun, and I sneer at people who sneer at summer movies—in fact, I sneer at people who sneer at entertainment for en-

tertainment's sake. I feel sorry for them, too. Riding that high horse has got to be uncomfortable, especially with a stick up your butt."
—*Entertainment Weekly*, August 20, 2004

"What I'm talking about is the difference between movies that are entirely entertainment, that exist just for that purpose, and pictures that also want to make us larger as human beings. But one of the things that I think makes us larger as human beings, or that improves our lives, is the ability to dream. To just dream. Why not? I mean, why does the dream have to be a socially conscious thing or anything like that? It can just be, you know, *The Road Warrior*."
—*Interview*, February 1986

"I love the movies. ... I love living those other lives for a while; I love those bright stories played out in the dark. And although my mental reach is longer than it was when I was 16, what I ask of movies hasn't changed much: Entertain me for a while. Touch my emotions without insulting my intelligence."
—*Entertainment Weekly*, December 24, 2004

"I love the movies. Let's get that up front. Have since I was a kid. And I'm from an unsophisticated school of thought that believes a movie (always a movie and never a film, even if it comes with subtitles) should be fun before it's anything else: an ice cream cone for the brain."
—*Entertainment Weekly*, August 20, 2004

"The mechanics of moviemaking and the mechanics of mufflers are of roughly equal interest to the general public. The difference is, the Midas man doesn't hand you a DVD along with his bill and say, 'I thought you might like to look at this at home. It's true I added a buck to the total, but there's an alternate ending where I leave off a bolt, and a deleted scene where I scrape my knuckles and yell some four-letter words. Plus the hilarious outtake where I give the front-end guy a wedgie."
—*Entertainment Weekly*, June 17, 2005

"Violence scares people, when something happens that's overtly violent. There's a place for that in the movies. It should be there."
—*Starburst*, 1983

"*Friday the 13th* is an immoral movie from my point of view; it's saying, 'Come in and watch people get killed.' It's like a porno novel, in which the writer of

this Beeline Original says, 'Come and read this book and you'll see people fuck and fuck and fuck and fuck!' ... That's what *Friday the 13th* does, except...well, basically, it's a snuff movie, isn't it? Simple as that."
—*The Boston Phoenix*, June 17, 1980

"I think that some of the people who go and see the hacker movies are also people who would like to go out and do that exact thing and don't have the guts to do it. That is to say, they would like to get a woman alone and probably— you know, some of them are pretty tabloidish films. They're pretty graphic and they're blunt. There don't seem to be any real twists. The worst one I ever saw was *The Toolbox Murders*. But there's a part of me that, well...there's a guy who gets a girl at one point with a nailer, one of these gadgets, right in the forehead. But there's a part of me that reacts to that and says, 'Oh, my God, that's awful. Let's do it again.'"
—*Starburst*, 1983

"It used to be that the sight of, you know, some guy fondling a bare breast was going to send the sixteen year olds of America out into the streets to rape the first thing that they saw in skirts, but the rating board no longer believes that. They believe that if you see a driver on a steamroller run over a guy, then the sixteen year olds of America are all going to go out and find steamrollers and run over their little brothers."
—*Boston Herald*, July 27, 1986

"Hollywood is caught in this double bind. They want gore, but you can't give 'em too much gore. They need an 'R,' because if they go unrated, they won't get any distribution."
—*Interview*, February 1986

"What happened to serious American movies? I ask because the best ones, such as *The Hurt Locker*, no longer get anything resembling a wide release, while Michael Bay's idiotic *Transformers 2* movie opened on 4,200 screens. That's a lot of space taken up by SFX and Megan Fox's perky breasts. And consider this: *Locker* cost about $11 million to make. It's a work of genius. *Revenge of the Fallen* had a budget almost 20 times that, and it's a work of crap."
—*Entertainment Weekly*, September 18, 2009

§

THE HORROR GENRE

"My fascination with the horror genre began with the E.C. comics of the early Fifties—my generation's *National Enquirer*—and with the horror movies of the Fifties, most notably *The Creature from the Black Lagoon*, *Invasion of the Body Snatchers*, *The Brain from Planet Arous*, and later the AIP creature features, which remain interesting to me because the best of them (although none of them was really very good) involved teenagers and took off into horror from such mundane settings."

—*Cinefantastique*, Winter 1978

"Is horror art? On this second level, the work of horror can be nothing else; it achieves the level of art simply because it is looking for something beyond art, something that predates art: it is looking for what I would call phobic pressure points. The good horror tale will dance its way to the center of your life and find the secret door to the room you believed no one but you knew of—as both Albert Camus and Billy Joel have pointed out, *The Stranger* makes us nervous... but we love to try on his face in secret."

—*Danse Macabre*, 1981

"Horror fiction has always had a reputation as an outlaw genre. It's thought of as kind of nasty, and when people see you reading *Salem's Lot* or something similar, there's a little bit of an attitude that you must be strange or warped."

—"An Evening with Stephen King at the Billerica," 1983

"When we talk about horror fiction we are always concentrating on certain outlaw elements of the genre; I think a lot of guys who write this stuff and direct the films—and I'm one of them, God knows—will try to pretty it up from time to time, in an effort to say to people in the press, 'Look, I'm not antisocial, I'm not anti-society or anything like that,' but...we're in the business of selling public executions here. People come by the droves. The same way that they used to come to Tower Hill to watch the executioner chop off people's heads—they want to see blood flow."
—*Den of Geek!*, May 13, 1983

"It doesn't hurt to emphasize again that horror fiction is a cold touch in the midst of the familiar, and good horror fiction applies this cold touch with a sudden, unexpected pressure. When we go home and shoot the bolt on the door, we like to think we're locking trouble out. The good horror story about the Bad Place whispers that we are not locking the world out; we are locking ourselves in...with them."
—*Danse Macabre*, 1981

"My own feeling about this is that almost all horror stories mirror specific areas of free-forming anxieties. And that sounds like a mouthful, a lot of intellectual bullshit, but what I mean is, when you read a horror novel or see a horror film, you make a connection with the things you're afraid of in your own life."
—*Twilight Zone*, April 1981

"To me it's sort of interesting, in World War II, the Universal monsters like Frankenstein, Wolf Man, Dracula, all disappear. There was enough real-life horror. And then, after World War II is over, you see the monsters start to come out of their dark holes again. And the biggest monster of them all was Godzilla from Japan, and he was caused by nuclear radiation. So you have a case of the first nuclear monster originating from the only people in the history of the world who have ever had to face the atomic bomb in a real-life situation. So we see entertainment, but we also see always this working out of the real fears that are underneath."
—*Nightline*, December 10, 1997

"In a lot of cases that's what the horror story is, it's like if you ever play pool, it's like when you kiss it off into the opposite pocket by banging it in a different direction. It doesn't solve anything, and people who think that it does are wrong. They say 'Well, you can confront your fears,' but as you pointed out, it's not exactly like that; to read a story about vampires is not really to confront one's fears, I believe, unless you're a superstitious peasant from the Carpathian mountains, who believes that there really are, seriously, beings who can live thousands and thousands of years by sucking blood."

—*Den of Geek!*, May 13, 1983

"Take the headline, 'Baby Nailed to Wall.' You say, 'I never did that to my kids, although I had the impulse a couple of times.' And that's where the horror is born."

—*Penthouse*, April 1982

"Horror is one of the ways we walk our imagination. It's a way to relieve bad feelings rather than something that causes them."

—*Detroit Free Press*, November 12, 1982

"I think that the horror story serves as an outlet or a catharsis for these deep-seated fears that are really about sex."

—*Twilight Zone*, April 1981

"Because books and movies are mass media, the field of horror has often been able to do better than even these personal fears over the last thirty years. During that period (and to a lesser degree, in the seventy or so years preceding), the horror genre has often been able to find national phobic pressure points, and those books and films which have been the most successful always seem to play upon and express fears which exist across a wide spectrum of people. Such fears, which are often political, economic, and psychological rather than supernatural, give the best work of horror a pleasing allegorical feel—and it's the one sort of allegory that most filmmakers seem at home with. Maybe because they know that if the shit starts getting too thick, they can always bring the monster shambling out of the darkness again."

—*Danse Macabre*, 1981

"People's spiritual lives always seem to fall into turmoil and the literature of the supernatural always becomes more prevalent (and more interesting) as the end of the century approaches. I don't know why it's so, but it is...you find your rationalists in the middle of the century, and your real good wars."
—*Cinefantastique*, Winter 1978

"Horror movies and horror novels have always been popular, but every ten or twenty years they seem to enjoy a cycle of increased popularity and visibility. These periods almost always seem to coincide with periods of fairly serious economic and/or political strain, and the books and films seem to reflect those free-floating anxieties (for want of a better term) which accompany such serious but not mortal dislocations. They have done less well in periods when the American people have been faced with outright examples of horror in their own lives."
—*Danse Macabre*, 1981

"My idea about the difference between humor and horror is that it stops being funny when it starts being you. If you see the Three Stooges and they're going boink, quack, quack, quack, it's funny. Except if somebody walked up to you and started going like that, it would be awful, particularly in public."
—*Inside*, April 4, 1986

§

IDEAS

"[P]eople ask, 'Where do you get your ideas?' That's the toughest one. Usually what I say is Utica, I get my ideas in Utica."
                    —"An Evening with Stephen King at the Billerica," 1983

"I get them from the lord Satan."
                    —Speech in Portland, Oregon, March 7, 1990

"I'll end up sitting [on an airplane] next to somebody who'll say 'Where do you get your ideas?' And I'll say, "Jesus Christ, I've never heard that one before, where do I get my...' But if you're at 40,000 feet and there's turbulence you know the last thing you want to be doing is answering that question again when the plane goes down."
                    —*Dennis Miller Live*, April 3, 1998

"At parties, people usually approach the writer of horror fiction with a mixture of wonder and trepidation. They look carefully into your eyes to make sure there's no overt bloodlust in them, and then ask the inevitable question: 'I really liked your last story...where do you get your ideas?' That question is common to any writer who works in a specialized genre, whether it's mystery, crime, western, or science fiction. But it's delivered in different tones for different fields. It's directed to the mystery writer with real admiration, the way you'd ask a magician how he sawed a lady in half. It's directed to the science fiction writer with honest respect for a fellow who is farseeing and visionary.

But it is addressed to the horror writer with a sense of fascinated puzzlement— the way a lady reporter might ask mild-mannered Henri Landru how it feels to do away with all those wives."
—*Writers Digest*, 1973

"Let's get one thing clear right now, shall we? There is no Idea Dump, no Story Central, no Island of the Buried Bestsellers; good ideas seem to come quite literally from nowhere, sailing at you right out of the empty sky: two previously unrelated ideas come together and make something new under the sun. Your job isn't to find these ideas but to recognize them when they show up."
—*On Writing*, 2000

"So where do the ideas—the salable ideas—come from? For myself, the answer is simple enough. They come from my nightmares. Not the nighttime variety, as a rule, but the ones that hide just beyond the doorway that separates the conscious from the unconscious. A good assumption to begin with is what scares you will scare someone else."
—*Writers Digest*, 1973

"People think the muse is a literary character, some cute little pudgy devil who floats around the head of the creative person sprinkling fairy dust. Well, mine's a guy with a flattop in coveralls who looks like Jack Webb and says, 'All right, you son of a bitch, time to get to work.'"
—*Time*, October 6, 1986

"I get inspiration, a lot of times, from very commonplace things that just strike a chord and develop themselves in the subconscious. Sometimes it's something a little bit more sensational than that. As an example, there is a story in the book *Night Shift* called 'The Mangler,' about a laundry machine that takes on a sort of malignant life. I worked in a laundry for about a year and a half after I got out of college. It was the only job I could find to support my wife and our first child. There was a fellow there that had no hands or forearms. He simply had hooks. This is one of the things that they don't tell you about when you become management: You have to wear a tie. It was this fellow's tie that did him in."
—*The Highway Patrolman*, July 1987

"The ideas come and they have to be let out, that's all. They just have to be let out."

—*60 Minutes*, February 16, 1997

"Working on a new idea is kind of like getting married. Then a new idea comes along and you think, 'Man, I'd really like to go out with her.' But you can't. At least not until the old idea is finished."

—*Los Angeles Herald*, January 31, 1989

"This has been an extremely fertile period for me in terms of ideas. I've had four or five in a row, all of which would make wonderful books or short stories or something. I know pretty much what they are. I told one to my wife the other day and she said: 'Gee, I think that one's really good. Are you going to write that down?' And I said: 'Well, I'm working on *Gerald's Game*.' And she said: 'I don't mean are you going to write the book, I mean are you going to write it down so you won't forget it?' And my response was: 'If you forget it, you never wanted to write it in the first place.'"

—*Writer's Digest*, March 1992

§

THE MEDIA

"With the enthusiastic collaboration of the American news media, the sideshow has somehow become the main attraction in American culture; the weirder the guy, the bigger the headlines. It's sickening that it takes a columnist in an entertainment magazine to point out that more than 2,000 newspeople covered the [Michael] Jackson trial—which is only a few hundred more than the number of American servicemen and women who have died in Iraq. On the same day that crowds gathered in Times Square (and around the world) to learn the fate of the Pale Peculiarity, another four suicide bombings took place in that tortured, bleeding country. And if you tell me that news doesn't belong in *Entertainment Weekly*, I respond by saying Michael Jackson under a black umbrella doesn't belong on the front page of the *New York Times*."
—*Entertainment Weekly*, June 14, 2005

"You know, this morning, the two big stories on CNN are Kanye West's mother, who died, apparently, having some plastic surgery. The other big thing that's going on is whether or not this cop [Drew Peterson] killed his wife. And meanwhile, you've got Pakistan in the midst of a real crisis, where these people have nuclear weapons that we helped them develop. You've got a guy in charge, who's basically declared himself the military strongman and is being supported by the Bush administration, whose raison d'etre for going into Iraq was to spread democracy in the world."
—*Time*, November 23, 2007

"As journalism it's immoral, and as entertainment, it's outright pimpery. Thirty-five years ago I wrote a novel called *The Running Man*, in which viewers watched fugitives run until they were executed on national television. I never expected to see anything remotely like it for real, but I never imagined Nancy Grace...and I've got a pretty nasty imagination."
—*Entertainment Weekly*, October 6, 2006

"As far as the yellow journalism goes, I just have utter contempt for that. That's taking people's most miserable fears and using them to turn a buck. That's terrible."
—*Famous Monsters*, April 1980

"[On Glenn Beck:] He reminds me of certain people you encounter in big cities. You know, the ones wearing robes, sandals, and signs proclaiming that the world is going to end because American men are eating too much red meat and American women are wearing their pants too tight. He's crazy, but—like those urban nutcakes—he actually seems to believe what he's saying."
—*Entertainment Weekly*, July 30, 2010

§

MONEY

"Luckily, the $400,000 didn't come all at once in small, unmarked bills. We could make the transition gradually, like a diver coming to the surface stage by stage so he won't get the bends. It wasn't like a rock star who goes from being broke one day to having a Rolls and a mansion the next."
—*Milwaukee Journal*, September 15, 1980

"The only thing that I do with money and the only thing I think money is any good for is to give you a little security. You have a roof over your head. You know your children are going to be fed. You know that they can go to school someplace that will fulfill their potential."
—*Inside*, April 4, 1986

"[W]hen people say, 'Do you write this kind of stuff for the money?' I say, 'No, I was always writing this kind of stuff.' The money found me, and I wouldn't want to kick it out. Anybody who throws money out the door has got to be nuts."
—*Twilight Zone*, April 1981

"The days when a check for some four-thousand-word wonder would buy penicillin for one of the kids' ear infections or help meet the rent are long gone. But the logic is more than spurious; it's dangerous. I don't exactly need the money the novels bring in, either, you see. If it was just the money, I could hang up my jock and hit the showers...or spend the rest of my life on some Caribbean island, catching the rays and seeing how long I could grow my fingernails."
—*Nightmares & Dreamscapes* (Introduction), 1992

"[On his four book $40 million contract:] The Bible says the laborer is worthy of his hire, so we took what we were offered."
—*Los Angeles Herald*, January 31, 1989

"I think you should be paid for what you do. Every morning, I wake up to the alarm clock, do my leg exercises, and then sit down at the word processor. By noon my back aches and I'm tired out. I work as hard or harder than I used to, so I want to be paid. But basically, at this point, it's how you keep score."
—*The Paris Review*, Fall 2006

"[Y]ou don't do it for money, or you're a monkey. You don't think of the bottom line, or you're a monkey. You don't think of it in terms of hourly wage, yearly wage, or even lifetime wage, or you're a monkey. In the end you don't even do it for love, although it would be nice to think so. You do it because to not do it is suicide."
—*Skeleton Crew* (Introduction), 1984

"I never wrote for money. People who write for money are not successes anyway. I wrote from love, and to get rid of whatever it was that kept me awake at night... I can't foresee a time when I would stop. But sooner or later, God tells you, 'You're out of the game, hang up your jock, that's it, you're through.'"
—*The Philadelphia Inquirer*, April 2, 1994

"[I]t's not the money. I'll admit I was bowled over to be paid $2,000 for 'Word Processor of the Gods,' but I was equally as bowled over to be paid $40 for 'The Reaper's Image' when it was published in *Startling Mystery Stories* or to be sent twelve contributor's copies when 'Here There Be Tygers' was published in *Ubris*..."
—*Skeleton Crew* (Introduction), 1984

"It used to be nobody would ever talk about sex and today the big no-no is money. Nobody's even supposed to admit that somebody earns money or that there is such a thing as money."
—*Inside*, April 4, 1986

"It's a little like being a free agent in baseball where you know everybody's saying, 'They paid X million dollars for this guy. We wanna see a home run every time he gets up.' Well, at least with a baseball bat he gets 450 at-bats a year, where I only get one. And it had better be a home run."
—*Los Angeles Herald*, January 31, 1989

"I could get those big advances, but I can do just fine without them. I made a decision when I left Viking that I'd ask to be made a partner in the publishing. Give me a modest amount to bind the deal over, and then we'll split the profits. Why not? It's still a good deal for them. But if I were doing it just for the money, I'd quit, because I've got enough."
—*The Paris Review*, Fall 2006

§

The Novel

"[W]hat always happens for me—with a book—is that you frame the idea of the book or the 'what if,' and little by little, characters will take shape. Generally as a result of a secondary decision about the plot."
—*Fangoria*, April 1984

"When you write a novel—well, at least for me, because I never think about theme as a starting point—I just think about the story. But sometimes, about three-quarters of the way through the first draft, you'll discover that there is a theme, or the potential for a theme. Or you discover what it is that you were actually talking about all along."
—*American Film*, June 1986

"I like to write three drafts: a first, a second, and what I think of as the editorial draft, when I sit down and take an editor's criticism and work it through in my mind, and put the whole book through the typewriter again, and repolish the other stuff as well."
—*Dream Makers: Volume II*, 1983

"I think, on a long piece of work, the key toward not falling out of love with it is to deepen what I know about the characters and get to like them better and to see around them through their eyes more."
—*Writer's Digest*, March 1992

"Suspense writers often disdain novels—and novelists—of ideas, so-called serious books and writers. Part of it is a very understandable inferiority complex that has been caused by the quick—and often unfair—dismissal of suspense novelists in the critical press, and part of it is a sincere feeling that most 'serious' novelists would be at a loss if asked to tell a suspenseful story, one that demands a strong situation and that the writer subordinate all other considerations to follow simple story values."
—John Fowles' *The Collector* (Introduction), 1989

"[N]ovels are still the best entertainment option. Even a hardcover is cheaper than two tickets to the local multiplex, especially once you throw in gas, parking, and babysitting. Also, a book lasts longer and there are no ads. Need more? No tiresome ratings system to keep you out if you're under 17, the special effects are always primo (because you make 'em up yourself), and although I read nearly 80 books this year, I never ran across the Olsen twins a single time."
—*Entertainment Weekly*, December 16, 2005

"Books are still very much a part of the total entertainment picture. They're portable, commercial-free, recyclable, and use no batteries. Also—unlike your Nintendo Game Boy—a book will rarely be taken away if you're discovered with one in study hall or even in the back row of math class. You can always claim it was for an assignment. Try getting away with that if you're discovered playing *Grand Theft Auto*. And finally, as Anthony Powell pointed out in 1971 (and the observation was not new with him), books do furnish a room."
—*Entertainment Weekly*, December 15, 2006

"Books have weight and texture; they make a pleasant presence in the hand. Nothing smells as good as a new book, especially if you get your nose right down in the binding, where you can still catch an acrid tang of the glue. The only thing close is the peppery smell of an old one. The odor of an old book is the odor of history, and for me, the look of a new one is still the look of the future."
—*Time*, June 19, 2000

§

OTHER WRITERS

"[T]here are a lot of people that I like a lot. I like Evan Hunter, who also writes under the name Ed McBain. There's a writer from Massachusetts, George Higgins, that I like a lot. I think he's good. John D. MacDonald, who writes mysteries. There's a guy who writes paperback originals, horror stories, Michael McDowell. I like his work. I like Peter Straub's writing a lot or I wouldn't have worked with him."

—"An Evening with Stephen King at the Billerica," 1983

"What I had to read in high school—their stuff—was dull old things like *Hamlet*, *Silas Marner*, *Moby-Dick* (alias *The Great White Bore*), and what seemed like hundreds of odd, elliptical poems by a Massachusetts spinster named Emily Dickinson. My stuff was what I read for love. It was more current, more vivid, and spoke with greater urgency about the world around me, a world that simultaneously intrigued and frightened me. I read John D. MacDonald's Travis McGee novels for love. I read Ed McBain's tales of the 87th Precinct for the same reason; I lived and died with detectives Carella, Kling, and especially Myer Myer, the cop who had two last names and worried so obsessively that he became totally bald."

—*Seventeen*, 1990

"The best horror novel I've read in about...well, I liked Peter Straub's *Ghost Story* very much. That's a good one. But the best horror novel that I've read in the last three years is Anne Rivers Siddons' book, *The House Next Door*."

—"Probabilities," September 8, 1979

"[On Clive Barker:] You read him with a book in one hand and an airsick bag in the other. That man is not fooling around. He's got a sense of humor, and he's not a dullard. He's better than I am now."
    —*Time*, October 6, 1986

"I was stunned by Mary Karr's memoir, *The Liar's Club*. Not just by its ferocity, its beauty, and by her delightful grasp of the vernacular, but by its totality—she is a woman who remembers everything about her early years."
    —*On Writing*, 2000

"*American Psycho* is a disturbing book. It's disturbing because it's very difficult for me to separate my feelings of revulsion about what's going on in the book, and the violence that's not just directed toward women—the violence in the book is directed toward the homeless, toward men, toward women, toward animals, across an entire spectrum. It's hard for me to separate that from my pervasive feeling that something is really going on in that book, that Bret Easton Ellis is trying very hard to express an entire attitude of an entire alienated culture... So my feelings about the book are ambivalent, but ambivalent on the downside."
    —Press conference, June 2, 1991

"Turns out Bret Easton Ellis is calling *Lunar Park* a Stephen King homage, and claims to have read *Salem's Lot* at least a dozen times as a kid... If Ellis really did read *Salem's Lot* a dozen times as a kid, the reasons for the past drug use he's spoken of become much clearer to me."
    —*Entertainment Weekly*, September 30, 2005

"I see a lot of books that must have been inspired by some of the stuff I'm doing. For one thing, those 'horror' novels that have gerund endings are just everywhere: *The Piercing, The Burning, The Searing*—the this-ing and the that-ing."
    —*Penthouse*, April 1982

"I have never been able to understand the prejudice some people seem to feel about recorded books, for instance. Not only are good stories better when they are told out loud; bad stories declare themselves almost at once, because the spoken word is merciless. You cannot, for instance, listen to one of the later

Patricia Cornwell novels without realizing how little feel she has for language, or to a Sue Grafton without appreciating her divine eye for the minutiae of ordinary life."
—*Entertainment Weekly*, January 25, 2008

"Audio is merciless. It exposes every bad sentence, half-baked metaphor, and lousy word choice. (Listen to a Tom Clancy novel on CD, and you will never, ever read another. You'll never be able to look at another one without gibbering.)"
—*Entertainment Weekly*, November 3, 2006

"There are a lot of books I wish I had written, but I guess maybe *The Grapes of Wrath* more than any of the other ones. Except maybe in *Light in August* by William Faulkner."
—*Inside*, April 4, 1986

"I wish I'd written *Lord of the Flies*. I love that book. People will ask, 'What's the first book that ever scared you?,' and that was the first book that ever really scared me. It terrified me."
—Q&A in Portland, Oregon, November 2, 2006

"Ray Bradbury was an influence. I read *The October Country*, and I've never forgotten the effect of great stories like 'The Jar' and 'The Crowd.'"
—*Twilight Zone*, April 1981

"In terms of reading, the early Bradbury played a part (although I did not discover him until my teens), the early Bloch, and a number of Forties paperback editions of Lovecraft that I found in an aunt's attic. Lovecraft struck me with the most force, and I still think, that for all his shortcomings, he is the best writer of horror fiction that America has yet produced."
—*Cinefantastique*, Winter 1978

"As a high school student I found Edgar Allen Poe a prolix, leather-lunged bore who was about as scary as the prize in a box of Cracker Jacks; I condemned Robert Frost as a pedestrian hick; considered Hemingway a macho jerk with an elephant gun where his heart should be."
—*Seventeen*, April 1990

"I think Richard Matheson is fantastic. When he's at his best, he has no peer."
—*Twilight Zone*, April 1981

"People always say to me, 'Well, what about H.P. Lovecraft?' And the thing was, you read Lovecraft when you were a kid but I never felt that he was speaking my language. It was chillier than my heart was, and when Matheson started to write about ordinary people and stuff, that was something that I wanted to do. I said, 'This is the way to do it. He's showing the way.'"
—*USA Weekend*, March 6-8, 2009

"I've learned a lot of my craft from the naturalistic writers, Theodore Dreiser and Frank Norris and people like that, and the idea that I picked up was 'Never back up, never flinch, never look away, see everything until you become this sort of disinterested observer."
—*Interview*, January 1986

"Mystery-suspense writer Michael Connelly is cool. So is George Pelecanos. Elmore Leonard, the true Daddy Cool of American letters, is chillier than your freezer's ice-cube dispenser. Robert Parker used to be cool but isn't anymore. Ditto Patricia Cornwell. James Patterson never was, never will be."
—*Entertainment Weekly*, November 16, 2007

"Both [J.K.] Rowling and [Stephenie] Meyer, they're speaking directly to young people... The real difference is that Jo Rowling is a terrific writer and Stephenie Meyer can't write worth a darn. She's not very good."
—*USA Weekend*, March 6-8, 2009

"I like to meet my peers, people like Peter Straub, Ramsey Campbell, Whitley Streiber. I like to sit around with these guys and shoot the shit and have a few beers."
—*Knave*, 1987

"If I have to spend time in purgatory before going to one place or the other, I guess I'll be all right as long as there's a lending library (if there is it's probably stocked with nothing but novels by Danielle Steel and *Chicken Soup* books, ha-ha, joke's on you, Steve)."
—*On Writing*, 2000

"If you asked me to name the best living American novelist, I'd probably come up with 50 names. I might be able to winnow the list down to a dozen, then I'd have a nervous breakdown. But ask me to name the best living novelist who's fierce, brave, funny, scatological, beautiful, convoluted, and paranoid—and who seems to feel that the real American Experience stopped happening right around the time Richard Nixon helicoptered away into obscurity—and it becomes simple: James Ellroy. If insanity illuminated by highly dangerous strokes of literary lightning is your thing, then Ellroy's your man."
—*Entertainment Weekly*, April 16, 2010

"[On his favorite suspense authors:] Ira Levin; Richard Matheson; Robert Bloch; these are the writers associated with my genre who seem to generate the most raw, sweaty-palmed suspense in me. But there are others, not always genre-related, who also do it: Daphne Du Maurier, Mary Higgins Clark (when she's telling a story that's on the mark and not ridiculous), Joseph Hayes, Thomas Chastain, Robert Parker, Jim Thompson, David Goodis, John Fowles, P.D. James, Ruth Rendell (the best suspense writer alive, I think), Robertson Davies…man, I could rock on all night. Oddly enough, the two best suspense novels I've ever read aren't 'horror' or 'mystery/suspense' novels at all. They are *The Lord of the Flies* by William Golding, and *The Sound of His Horn*, by a French fellow named only Sarban."
—*Mystery Scene*, 1987

"Somebody who's a terrific writer who's been very, very successful is Jodi Picoult. You've got Dean Koontz, who can write like hell. And then sometimes he's just awful. It varies. James Patterson is a terrible writer but he's very, very successful."
—*USA Weekend*, March 6-8, 2009

§

POLITICS

"It can be argued that Kennedy was the last president to be elected pretty much without TV being the overmastering factor. So that once TV began, there were no more good presidents. And every time we elect a new president, we get farther away from real politics and real people and more into the world of guest-of-the-week on *Three's Company*."
—*Penthouse*, April 1982

"I think that a lot of so-called Yuppies decided they didn't have any souls to search, so the hell with it, and that a lot of what you see now is a kind of soulless reaction to the Sixties. After all, we didn't get much out of that whole routine. The only President that spoke for our sort of ideals and our feelings was shot down like a dog in the street. The prime speaker for human rights, Martin Luther King, was shot down like a dog in the street. Bobby Kennedy was shot down in a hotel kitchen or something like that. So one of the lessons that we learned through those things and through Vietnam was that if there's somebody you don't like or if there's a philosophy you don't agree with, shoot those people, and that will take care of that problem."
—*Amazing Authors Showcase*, 1988

"Kennedy was the last guy that I truly supported, and I was too young to vote. I voted for Dukakis, I voted for Mondale, I voted for Carter when he ran against Reagan. I voted for Carter the year he won; I guess that's the closest I've ever come, except Carter turned out not really to be a winner."
—*Amazing Authors Showcase*, 1988

"I have a friend who claims that the devil was in Lyndon Johnson. 'The devil entered Lyndon Johnson when he became president and forced him to do all those awful things in Vietnam.' And this guy says that when Johnson went on TV after the New Hampshire primary and wouldn't stand for reelection, that he actually saw the devil leave Johnson's face. I wonder if there isn't a lot of truth in that."
—*High Times*, January 1981

"My wife still delights in telling people that her husband cast his first Presidential ballot, at the tender age of twenty-one, for Richard Nixon. 'Nixon said he had a plan to get us out of Vietnam,' she says, usually with a gleeful gleam in her eye, 'and Steve believed him!'"
—*Nightmares & Dreamscapes* (Introduction), 1992

"People pick up *Salem's Lot* and read about vampires. Vampires seem optimistic compared to Ronald Reagan, who is our American version of a vampire, of the living dead. I mean Reagan's real, he's a real person, but vampires look good next to him because you know that you can at least dismiss the vampires when the movie's over or when you close the book."
—*Sounds*, May 21, 1983

"[Bill Clinton] has clearly got serious problems with controlling his sexual urges. I don't think that this is a substantive issue in his presidency, and basically there are a lot of right-wing groups in this country that want to see him impeached for adultery. I'm sorry, adultery is not an impeachable offense. The lying that he did was the sort of lying that anybody does when they've been caught in an embarrassing sexual situation. And that's not substantive in terms of his constitutional duties. Ken Starr is an odious little man who is trying to justify all the money that he's spent by finding anything that's dirty on this guy. And God knows, sexually speaking, Clinton's hands are not clean. But the American people knew what he was when they hired him."
—*Salon*, September 24, 1998

"The foreign press around the world will look at the situation we're going through right now and their reaction—and that of a lot of American people, including myself—is to throw up your hands and say, 'Oh, please—get over it. This is a juvenile preoccupation. People are starving in Africa. People are killing each other in Africa. Stop worrying about Monica Lewinsky's thong panties.'"

—*Salon*, September 24, 1998

"What really makes me insane is how eager politicians are to use pop culture—not just videogames but TV, movies, even *Harry Potter*—as a whipping boy. It's easy for them, even sort of fun, because the pop-cult always hollers nice and loud. Also, it allows legislators to ignore the elephants in the living room. Elephant One is the ever-deepening divide between the haves and have-nots in this country, a situation guys like Fiddy and Snoop have been indirectly rapping about for years. Elephant Two is America's almost pathological love of guns. It was too easy for critics to claim—falsely, it turned out—that Cho Seung-Hui (the Virginia Tech killer) was a fan of *Counter-Strike*; I just wish to God that legislators were as eager to point out that this nutball had no problem obtaining a 9mm semiautomatic handgun. Cho used it in a rampage that resulted in the murder of 32 people. If he'd been stuck with nothing but a plastic videogame gun, he wouldn't even have been able to kill himself."

—*Entertainment Weekly*, April 11, 2008

"[On visiting England:] I've never done Europe. I think in a way, with the world situation like it is, England's bad enough. I feel like I ought to wear a shirt saying, 'I didn't vote for [Bush]. He's not my guy. Don't blame me.' I think he's an idiot. But then I think Blair's an idiot, too, so there."

—*The Times*, October 21, 2006

"I didn't have any opinion on Tony Blair at all until he kissed—you know—it seemed he became almost like a puppet on George's knee. I mean, that's how he comes across. I'm sure he's not. It seems like, in the joint press conferences, Tony is always the guy who seems to be saying, 'Now George, isn't this what you really mean?' He seems much more articulate [like] somebody who actually has some brains, whereas George doesn't seem to have much. Luckily I'm not the Dixie Chicks and my constituency probably won't repudiate me for saying that. If they do, they do."

—*The Times*, October 21, 2006

"[On George W. Bush:] My wife has a bumper sticker on the back of the car that says, 'Somewhere in Texas a village is missing its idiot.'"

—*The Times*, October 21, 2006

"We need a big change. It's an amazing thing to see the two frontrunners be a woman and a black man. Obama has the least baggage of the two and is willing to try new things. It wouldn't be business as usual. Also it would do wonders for us in the world community to have a black man in the White House."

—*The Berkshire Eagle*, January 21, 2008

"I've got an Obama sticker on my car, and I guess that says what needs saying. Call me a tiresome liberal if you want, but I just think it would be nice to have a smart guy running things for a change. We tried dumb and it hasn't worked out too well."

—StephenKing.com, September 4, 2008

"I hail from a family of rock-ribbed Republicans (my grandfather disliked FDR so much he only referred to him as "that fool in the White House"), but I got pushed left during the idiocy that was Vietnam and have been voting Democrat ever since. My euphoria over the election of Barack Obama was only surpassed by my pleasure in knowing Dubya was back in Texas, where could do no further damage."

—*Entertainment Weekly*, February 20, 2009

§

Popular Culture

"If you like Celine Dion, you should write or e-mail the editors of this magazine and tell them that on no account should they hire Steve King to write commentaries, because Steve King thinks 'Who Let the Dogs Out' is better than all the songs Ms. Dion has recorded, put together."
—*Entertainment Weekly*, August 8, 2003

"Radio, and in particular, music, made me real as a kid. It's where I discovered my identity. You reach out and find something that belongs to you and it's yours. It's difficult to explain, but it's like a pair of shoes that fit you. My first record was a 78 rpm version of Elvis Presley's 'Hound Dog.' From that moment on I knew it's what I wanted, and I wanted all I could get."
—*Radio and Records*, 1984

"Ask me to name the greatest rock & roll song of all time and I have to say it's a three-way tie between Slobberbone's 'Gimme Back My Dog,' Count Five's 'Psychotic Reaction,' and Elvis Costello's '(What's So Funny 'Bout) Peace, Love and Understanding.' What I'm not interested in is ear candy. There's a place where you can put that, and it's not in your ear. I think that stuff should crawl right out of the radio speaker and get in your face."
—*Entertainment Weekly*, August 8, 2003

"For me, rock and roll was the rise of consciousness. It was like a big sun bursting over my life. That's when I really started to live—and that was brought on by the music of the Fifties."
—*Twilight Zone*, February 1984

"Is anything more depressing than hearing late-'60s, early-'70s counterculture anthems co-opted for TV ads? Every time I hear Led Zeppelin's 'Rock and Roll' on a Cadillac commercial, I think my head is going to explode. Do advertisers think the boomers are still reliving Woodstock? And dear God, could they be right?"
—*Entertainment Weekly*, January 13, 2006

"The place that used to rock (when you could get away from Karen Carpenter and the Cowsills, anyway) was the radio. Then the hit-making machinery kind of got lost in a welter of bad rap, dull boy bands, and vocalists—both male and female—who all sounded like Michael Jackson. If you wanted rock, you had to find a so-called classic-rock station...and I should know, I own one. The trouble with classic rock is that you can only listen to Aerosmith sing 'Walk This Way' so many times without wanting to run the other way. (But it still beats Kelly Clarkson.)"
—*Entertainment Weekly*, April 30, 2004

"I think there ought to be some serious discussion by smart people, really smart people, about whether or not proliferation of things like The Smoking Gun and TMZ and YouTube and the whole celebrity culture is healthy. We've switched from a culture that was interested in manufacturing, economics, politics—trying to play a serious part in the world—to a culture that's really entertainment-based. I mean, I know people who can tell you who won the last four seasons of *American Idol* and they don't know who their Congressmen are."
—*Time*, November 23, 2007

"Pop culture is full of pleasures, but it also has its share of annoyances; for every pretty, talented Elisha Cuthbert there is a Paris Hilton (and her little dog, too)."
—*Entertainment Weekly*, October 29, 2004

"What I'm asking is whether this is still a country where a peculiar person such as Michael Jackson can get a fair shake and be considered innocent until proven guilty...or is this just a 21st-century American barnyard where we all feel free to turn on the moonwalking rooster...and peck it to death?"
—*Entertainment Weekly*, February 13, 2004

"I think of Columnist Hell as either an eternity of Larry King interviews or a never-ending *American Idol* audition in Memphis. Dig the pain: damned to converse with Paula Abdul between acts...forever."
—*Entertainment Weekly*, February 16, 2007

§

The Publishing Industry

"I heard one member of the top brass [at Doubleday] once say he'd like to get every agent in New York and blow their knees off with a shotgun. It's that kind of an outfit."
—Starship, Spring 1981

"There are times when I feel a little bit irritated at the publishers, who seem to think that the tour is a necessary adjunct to bestsellerdom. Or who have somehow got the idea, that publishers didn't used to have, that if your books sell well you ought to be some kind of celebrity, that that's yours by right, that you must want it."
—Penthouse, April 1982

"What can paperback publishers do? The obvious answer is not in-book advertising or independent production (which, in the movie business, has led not to the encouragement of creativity, but to a repetitive series of sexy teenpix, slasher films, and neo-war movies) but a mind change. This is very traumatic for book people; they think well, but are innovative as a last resort."
—Publishers Weekly, December 20, 1985

"I'll take less [money] but it doesn't make a goddamn bit of difference. They just give it to each other in salaries and hire two or three more supernumeraries to fill worthless positions. They are the most uninformed, asinine bunch in American business... I mean here we have a business that is basically the business of American thought and it's very influential. And yet in a financial sense we rank just below the brassiere makers in terms of the input into the gross

national product. We're not in the Fortune 500. Publishing is not one of the big American industries. And yet it certainly has a much more potent input into American life and the American course of the future than, say, the bra makers. Although the bra makers do have some, of course."
—*Miami Herald*, March 25, 1984

"Publishing houses, once proudly independent, are today little more than corporate wampum beads, their cultural clout all but gone. Novels that were neither dopey best-sellers (think James Patterson) nor dull 'serious fiction' (think William Gaddis, Paul Auster, and their overpraised ilk) were one of the first things to go when the conglomerates took over. Dull or dopey: These days that's pretty much your choice at the bookstore."
—*Entertainment Weekly*, September 11, 2003

"There are no marketing surveys done—there has not been an industry-wide marketing survey since 1968. So they run on inertia. It's a gentleman's business, and they have to run it like gentlemen and gentlemen don't get their hands dirty with things like market analysis."
—*Miami Herald*, March 25, 1984

"Recent publishing history is full of worthy novels that were published only by the skin of their teeth. J.K. Rowling's maiden *Harry Potter* voyage was one. Then there's the sad case of John Kennedy Toole's *A Confederacy of Dunces*, published only after the despairing author had killed himself. (It then reached the best-seller list, which may or may not have been of some comfort to his surviving relatives.) The moral? It's a jungle out there, baby, and in a world where the corporate bottom line is god (or maybe the word I'm searching for is mammon), the strong survive but the worthy often do not."
—*Entertainment Weekly*, September 11, 2003

"I believe that 70 percent of the fiction and nonfiction best-seller lists is dreck, and that *The Da Vinci Code*, by Dan Brown, stands as a prime example."
—*Entertainment Weekly*, August 8, 2003

"It occurs to me that publishers may confuse 'selling' with 'pimping.' If so, here's a flash: They're not the same. Sell this one, and you make it possible for this guy to write the next one. You're doing him a mitzvah. And not just him.

What about the ordinary reader? In case you forgot, guys, we are your friends, not unwashed, unlettered, germ-laden interlopers at the literary feast."
—*Entertainment Weekly*, April 6, 2007

"You know as well as I do that publishers, music publishers, studio heads, they could not give a shit for the writer, the creator. They care about their bankbooks and that's about all they care about."
—*The Guardian*, September 14, 2000

"I can't imagine retiring from writing. What I can imagine doing is retiring from publishing."
—*Time*, April 1, 2002

"[On the specialty publishers:] I expect him to come to me and say I want a limited edition of 12 copies made of the skin of the unborn dick dick bird or something like that and I'd better ask $5,000 per copy, because these people are out of control."
—*The Times*, October 21, 2006

"A lot of the stuff that got published from the mid-Eighties to the Nineties was real shit. It deserves to be closed out. This is not the fault of the writers, it's always the fault of the publishers who extend contracts—especially when they're fairly lucrative ones, for bad writing that should fly as paperback originals, and most of it not even as that. Bad drives out good, and eventually the publishers look around and say, 'This stuff isn't selling.' You and I both know that what isn't selling is crap. It's what never sold. Sooner or later some time will go by and a *Green Mile* will come along, or a *Desperation*, or *The Exorcist*, or a *Rosemary's Baby*, and then all these know-nothings will turn around and go, 'Oh, horror is hot!' Then they'll start buying the bad novels again."
—*The World of Fandom*, 1996

§

Random Observations

"If you are telling the truth, then it seems to me that if somebody—some nut—does something based on what you wrote, all you can say is that this nut was too unoriginal to think up his own method of killing somebody, so he had to use what was in the book."

—*Penthouse*, April 1982

"There are other worlds than these. Fiction is crafted to discuss just those questions why we're here, the difference between predestination and randomness."

—*The Observer*, August 9, 1998

"I'm always convinced that the flatbed trucks, the big ones that have these tarpaulins over whatever's on the back of them…could be alien communicators or disruptors. For a long time I've been curious whether or not there are outbreaks of violence wherever a lot of these things are seen, because maybe aliens turn these things on and make people crazy."

—"An Evening with Stephen King at the Billerica," 1983

"*Misery* was just two characters in a bedroom, but *Gerald's Game* goes that one better—one character in a bedroom. I was thinking that eventually there's going to be another book that will just be called "Bedroom." There won't be any characters at all."

—*The Paris Review*, Fall 2006

"Whenever anyone says 'gratuitous violence,' what they mean is that someone showed us what it was really like, what those foot-pounds mean when they translate out of a fucking physics book and into the real world."
　　　—*Penthouse*, April 1982

"Violence for the sake of violence is of course immoral and thus pornographic; to shy away from a violent scene necessary to the story is equally immoral and equally pornographic."
　　　—*Mystery Scene*, 1987

"Most humor is based on somebody being hurt in some way, and we laugh at it, because thank God it isn't us."
　　　—*Cinefantastique*, September-October 1982

"One question that's been troubling me since Rob Reiner's *Stand by Me* came out almost 20 years ago: If Superman and Mighty Mouse duked it out, who'd win? According to Teddy Duchamp in the movie, the answer's a no-brainer: Superman, because Mighty Mouse is just a cartoon. And yet I wonder. Both are fictional characters, after all, and Mighty Mouse is obviously smaller and quicker."
　　　—*Entertainment Weekly*, January 13, 2006

"I think that this idea about the end of the world is very liberating. ... It's the end of all the shit, and you don't have to be afraid anymore, because the worst has already happened."
　　　—*Penthouse*, April 1982

"This is a dreadful thing to say, but I have wondered in my darker hours that, if everything were legal, wouldn't it be kind of a Darwinian solution to a lot of problems? Who are the bikies that you see who are cruisin' around with no helmet on with a hat turned around like that yoyo in Cheap Trick? They're dummies, and if they splatter their brains all over the sidewalk, they're not going to be collecting food stamps."
　　　—*High Times*, January 1981

"I taught school and you could see the students losing their imagination right in front of your eyes. I don't know whether it's peer pressure or some sort of governor they have. But imagination shrinks and shrinks and shrinks."
　　　—*Toronto Star*, October 5, 1983

"I sympathize with the losers of the world and to some degree understand the blind hormonal rage and ratlike panic which sets in as one senses the corridor of choice growing ever narrower, until violence seems like the only possible response to the pain. And although I pity the Columbine shooters, had I been in a position to do so, I like to think I would have killed them myself, if that had been the only choice; put them down the way one puts down any savage animal that cannot stop biting."
    —VEMA keynote address, May 26, 1999

"Book lovers are the Luddites of the intellectual world. I can no more imagine their giving up the printed page than I can imagine a picture in the New York Post showing the Pope technoboogieing the night away in a disco."
    —*Time*, June 19, 2000

"The keepers of the idea of serious literature have a short list of authors who are going to be let inside, and too often that list is drawn from people who know people, who go to certain schools, who come up through certain channels of literature. And that's a very bad idea—it's constraining for the growth of literature."
    —*Pittsburgh Post-Gazette*, October 31, 2006

"Fantasy is to the human mind what salt is to the diet. If you don't use your imagination, imagination will use you."
    —*Milwaukee Journal*, September 15, 1980

"I don't talk about this much, because it embarrasses me and it sounds pompous, but I still see stories as a great thing, something which not only enhances lives but actually saves them. Nor am I speaking metaphorically. Good writing—good stories—are the imagination's firing pin, and the purpose of the imagination, I believe, is to offer us solace and shelter from situations and life-passages which would otherwise prove unendurable."
    —*Nightmares & Dreamscapes* (Introduction), 1992

"Evil, let's face it, has a certain flash that good just doesn't have. Particularly for readers and viewers who are voyeurs by nature and who are generally attracted to things that they know they themselves will never be or couldn't do."
    —*Fangoria*, August 1986

"I try to make ordinary people seem ordinary, but yet I think most people are mainly good. I feel that way about people, even when I see them on the street; that they probably have something inside them that's decent, you know?"
—*Famous Monsters*, April 1980

"I think that any kind of story where something really terrible happens makes your own life look better by comparison. They give us a scale, to measure our own problems by."
—*Time*, April 1, 2002

"[S]ooner or later it will happen. We've seen so many false alarms—Y2K, the Avian Flu—and there's a tendency to say, 'Well, it's all bullshit, it'll be fine.' One of these days, though, it really is going to be the Spanish Flu again, and it's going to kill people. I do have some predictive powers—I mean, I'm the guy who wrote *The Running Man*, where the guy ends up crashing a jetliner into a New York skyscraper at the end of the book."
—*GQ*, May 7, 2009

"The interviews that I dread are, 'I'm going to ask you a lot of questions you've never heard before.' You know somehow, at that point, that they're going to ask you all the questions you've heard before."
—*Fangoria*, April 1984

"Some authors write things which must appeal to the directorial eye, that's all I can think of. I think there aren't very many novelists in this country under forty who are writing novels; they're all writing movies. It isn't anything as simple as the canard of writing dialogue and stage direction, but of seeing things in image after image, which is what good movies do."
—*Take One*, January 1979

"If someone were to ask me who I hate more, Bucky Dent or the Ayatollah Khomeini, I'd have to think about it."
—*Bangor Daily News*, October 6, 1980

"There's another conclusion to be drawn, too. 'You can lead a horse to water,' my mother used to tell me, 'but you can't make him drink.' I have since discovered that you can lead a kid to culture, but you can't make him or her think. You can't legislate Kesey in place of King, or Steinbeck in place of Steel; kids are going to go right on reading for love, and God love them for it. Thinking is one thing, love is another; both are important; they do not always exist together. If I had a dime for every book I read below the teacher's sight line, I could buy a car. They wanted me to walk placidly and look at the sights; I wanted to run, to dance up the walls like Fred Astaire."

—*Seventeen*, 1990

"I sometimes think that I'm a little more sloppy than I was. You get some of these old guy habits, you know (in an old man's voice): 'Don't tell me how to make this hat, boy. I've been making these hats since from when you were in your mother's womb. I know what I'm doing,' and the hat doesn't have any brim or the thing's inside out."

—*Writer's Digest*, March 1992

"I think [Florida is] where pop novelists go to die, in a way. It does feel a little like retirement now, but why not? I'm 60 now, so I can kick back a little bit. Sixty's the new 50, and dead is the new alive."

—*Time*, January 17, 2008

"Remembering where you were and what you were doing when you found out your first novel had been accepted for publication is as easy as remembering where you were on Pearl Harbor Day or on November 22, 1963—although the circumstances are much more pleasant."

—*Book-of-the-Month Club News*, October 1986

§

Richard Bachman

"Between 1977 and 1984 I published five novels under the pseudonym of Richard Bachman. These were *Rage* (1977), *The Long Walk* (1979), *Roadwork* (1981), *The Running Man* (1982), and *Thinner* (1984). There were two reasons I was finally linked to Bachman: first, because the first four books, all paperback originals, were dedicated to people associated with my life, and second, because my name appeared on the copyright forms of one book. Now people are asking me why I did it, and I don't seem to have any satisfactory answers. Good thing I didn't murder anyone, isn't it?"

—*The Bachman Books*, 1985

"I wrote under a pseudonym for two reasons: First, because I had a number of books in manuscript that I thought were fairly good and I was afraid of flooding the market with 'Stephen King' books. I didn't want to see them just moldering in a drawer, so the pen name seemed like a good compromise. Second, I wanted to see if I could achieve the same sort of success under another name that I had achieved as Stephen King."

—*Cosmopolitan*, December 1985

"I wanted to see what was in the name, but I also wanted to publish those books. They thought I would clog the market. They weren't really Stephen King books as it was then understood, they were short for a start."

—*The Guardian*, September 14, 2000

"I've been asked several times if I did it because I feel typecast as a horror writer. The answer is no. I don't give a shit what people call me as long as I can go to sleep at night."

—*The Bachman Books*, 1985

"There was growing speculation over the last three years that I was Bachman. Finally, a young bookstore employee in Washington, D.C., named Steve Brown, checked in the Library of Congress; the earliest Bachman book had copyright notice filed under my name—enough evidence to shoot a very large hole in the alias. I decided that further denials would be useless. The photograph on the jacket is of a man named Richard Manuel, a Minnesotan and an old friend of my agent's."

—*Cosmopolitan*, December 1985

"I was pissed [when I was outed as Bachman]. It's like you can't have anything. You're not allowed to because you're a celebrity. What does it matter? Why should anyone care? It's like they can't wait to find stuff out, particularly if it's something you don't want people to know. That's the best. That's the juice. It makes me think about that old Don Henley song, 'Dirty Laundry.' Hell, give it to them."

—*Maryland Coast Dispatch*, August 8, 1986

"It should have been in *Time*'s Milestones. Died. Richard Bachman, of cancer of the pseudonym."

—*Time*, October 6, 1986

"But the fact that *Thinner* did 28,000 copies when Bachman was the author and 280,000 copies when Steve King became the author, might tell you something, huh?"

—*The Bachman Books*, 1985

"Obviously, I'm Richard Bachman, and when I write as Richard Bachman it opens this part of my mind. It's like this hypnotic suggestion where I become my idea of who Richard Bachman is. It frees me to be somebody who is a little bit different. In a way *The Regulators* and *Desperation* are really different books, however what makes them interesting isn't the differences but the similarities."

—*The World of Fandom*, 1996

§

SHORT STORIES
AND NOVELLAS

"I like to write short stories more [than novels] because I never met a writer who wasn't lazy. And a short story is, by its very definition, short. It is something that generally you can turn out in a week to two weeks depending on how well it goes for you. But at the same time, it gives the same satisfaction of creating a complete world."
        —*The Highway Patrolman*, July 1987

"The four stories in *Different Seasons* were written for love, not money, usually in between other writing projects. They have a pleasant, open-air feel, I think—even at the grimmest moments there's something about them, I hope, that says the writer was having a good time, hanging loose, worrying not about the storyteller but only the tale."
        —*Booknotes*, August 1983

"I've continued to write short stories over the years, partly because the ideas still come from time to time—beautifully compressed ideas that cry out for three thousand words, maybe nine thousand, fifteen thousand at the very most—and partly because that's the way I affirm, at least to myself, the fact that I haven't sold out, no matter what the more unkind critics may think. Short stories are still piecework, the equivalent of those one-of-a-kind items you can buy in an artisan's shop. If, that is, you are willing to be patient and wait while it's made by hand in the back room."
        —*Everything's Eventual* (Introduction), 2001

"Writing short stories hasn't gotten easier for me over the years; it's gotten harder. The time to do them has shrunk, for one thing. They keep wanting to bloat, for another (I have a real problem with bloat—I write like fat ladies diet). And it seems harder to find the voice for these tales—all too often the I-Guy just floats away."
        —*Skeleton Crew* (Introduction), 1984

"I think I have succeeded in keeping my craft new, at least to myself, mostly because I refuse to let a year go by without writing at least one or two of them. Not for money, not even precisely for love, but as a kind of dues-paying. Because if you want to write short stories, you have to do more than think about writing short stories. It is not like riding a bicycle but more like working out in the gym; your choice is to use it or lose it."
        —*Everything's Eventual* (Introduction), 2001

"I still don't believe critics of the short story who say the O. Henry ending is inherently bad. You remember *The Twilight Zone* where the guy finally had enough time to read and he broke his glasses? There's nothing wrong with that."
        —*Twilight Zone*, December 1985

"Now, artistically speaking, there's nothing at all wrong with the novella. Of course, there's nothing wrong with circus freaks, either."
        —*Different Seasons* (Afterword), 1982

"If you can't write anything longer than a short story, don't push it (or try to pad it). In writing as in sex, the best advice is to relax and let nature take her course."
        —*Today*, January 22, 2008

§

STANLEY KUBRICK
AND *THE SHINING*

"[Kubrick] wants to hurt people. He wants to make a movie that people will be afraid to go see. ... I think he's going to try to make a picture so scary that it'll make *Alien* look like *Romper Room.*"
— *Nashville Tennesseean*, May 5, 1980

"You have to understand that my script was done before anybody had any idea that Kubrick would want to do the picture. I think that they might have gone ahead with my screenplay had it been somebody else."
— *Cinefantastique*, September-October 1982

"I have my days when I think that I gave Kubrick a live grenade which he heroically threw his body on."
— "An Evening with Stephen King at the Billerica," 1983

"[Kubrick's] not a pinhead, but also I don't have any reaction to him doing the book, primarily because I don't believe he has any real reaction to my work. It's a question of having read the book and saying, 'We can do certain things with this.'"
— "Probabilities," September 8, 1979

"[C]ertainly there are missed opportunities to scare the shit out of the audience. The question I really have is, did Kubrick know what he wanted? Or put it another way; did he know how to get what he wanted?"
— *The Boston Phoenix*, June 17, 1980

"It's very funny to me that [Kubrick] chose a hedge maze, because my original concept was to create a hedge maze. And the reason that I rejected the idea in favor of the topiary animals was because of an old Richard Carlson film, *The Maze*."

—*Cinefantastique*, Winter 1978

"Jack Nicholson, though a fine actor, was all wrong for the part. His last big role had been *One Flew Over the Cuckoo's Nest*, and between that and his manic grin, the audience automatically identified him as a loony from the first scene. But the book is about Jack Torrance's gradual descent into madness... If the guy is nuts to begin with, then the entire tragedy of his downfall is wasted. For that reason, the film has no center and no heart, despite its brilliantly unnerving camera angles and dazzling use of the Steadicam."

—*Playboy*, June 1983

"Too cold. No sense of emotional investment in the family whatsoever on his part. I felt that the treatment of Shelley Duvall as Wendy—I mean, talk about insulting to women. She's basically a scream machine. There's no sense of her involvement in the family dynamic at all. And Kubrick didn't seem to have any idea that Jack Nicholson was playing the same motorcycle psycho that he played in all those biker films he did—*Hells Angels on Wheels*, *The Wild Ride*, *The Rebel Rousers*, and *Easy Rider*. The guy is crazy. So where is the tragedy if the guy shows up for his job interview and he's already bonkers? No, I hated what Kubrick did with that."

—*The Paris Review*, Fall 2006

"It wasn't scary. I didn't like Nicholson in it doing predictable Nicholson schtick."

—*The Toronto Star*, February 8, 1997

"I would have rather seen Michael Moriarty or Martin Sheen portray Torrance. But these actors are not supposed to be 'bankable'—Hollywood loves that word."

—*Cinefantastique*, Winter 1978

"From a plotting level, I don't think the film works very well, and in terms of execution I think some of the choices he made about where to set his camera and how to shoot certain scenes were amazingly bad. And I know it must sound...not just pretentious, but downright...almost arrogant for me to say that because he's a great filmmaker and I've never even...you know, yelled 'cut' at the

end of a scene or anything. And it is pretentious, it is arrogant, and yet from the standpoint of film-goer; any film-goer who's seen enough films turns into a film critic, even if it's only in their own mind."
—*Den of Geek!*, May 13, 1983

"The novel was about a sane guy who goes crazy. The movie was about a crazy guy who goes totally bonkers. I had a problem with that."
—*The Cable Guide*, May 1990

"I thought that the real problem with *The Shining* was that Kubrick didn't have a real background in the genre. He wanted to make a horror film, it was the stated idea to make the scariest horror film of all time. He's a fantastic director, and I thought, 'Okay, they're going to have ambulances out in front of every theater in America, because they're going to bring people out to cardiac units!' It's a tremendously interesting film, but at the same time it seems to me like a great big luxury car with no motor in it."
—*Larry King Live*, April 10, 1986

"I think it's marvelous to look at, but Kubrick wanted to make a horror movie. And he made *The Shining* and what I felt was that he made the movie in a total vacuum, with no understanding of the basics of the genre."
—*Fangoria*, August 1986

"It's certainly beautiful to look at: gorgeous sets, all those Steadicam shots. I used to call it a Cadillac with no engine in it. You can't do anything with it except admire it as sculpture. You've taken away its primary purpose, which is to tell a story. The basic difference that tells you all you need to know is the ending. Near the end of the novel, Jack Torrance tells his son that he loves him, and then he blows up with the hotel. It's a very passionate climax. In Kubrick's movie, he freezes to death."
—*The Paris Review*, Fall 2006

"There are some parts of [the film] that I liked, and some parts that I didn't like at all. If you add it all up, it comes out to a zero."
—*Twilight Zone*, April 1981

"Director Stanley Kubrick had no idea what *The Shining* was about—he did things that *Friday the 13th* producers wouldn't do."
—*The Los Angeles Times*, 1985

"I would do everything different."
—*American Film*, June 1986

"Please believe me: nobody has a Freudian view of the relationship of man to his society. Not you, not me, not Kubrick, nobody. The whole concept is abysmally silly. And as a moviegoer, I don't give a tin whistle what the director thinks; I want to know what he sees. Most directors have good visual and dramatic instincts (most good directors, anyway), but in intellectual terms, they are pinheads, by and large. Nothing wrong in that; who wants a film director who's a utility infielder? Let them do their job, enjoy their work, but for Christ's sake, let's not see Freudianism in the work of any film director."
—*Cinefantastique*, Winter 1978

"The movie has no heart; there's no center to that picture. I wrote the book as a tragedy, and if it was a tragedy, it was because all the people loved each other. Here, it seems there's no tragedy because there's nothing to be lost."
—*The Boston Phoenix*, June 17, 1980

"I thought it was boring. If you go back and read the reviews when it was released, most of the critics thought it was boring too."
—*Indie London*, 2003

"I'm sorry, I go on about that, because there are other things...the atmosphere of the film, and the angles, the steadicam work, the hotel itself...using the hedge maze instead of the hedge animals in the book was probably a mistake, but though I also think the hedge maze was an interesting idea, I don't think it was used very well."
—*Den of Geek!*, May 13, 1983

"I'd like to remake *The Shining* someday, maybe even direct it myself if anybody will give me enough rope to hang myself with."
—*Playboy*, June 1983

§

SUCCESS

"Both creatively and financially, *Carrie* was a kind of escape hatch for Tabby and me, and we were able to flee through it into a totally different existence. Hell, our lives changed so quickly that for more than a year afterward, we walked around with big, sappy grins on our faces, hardly daring to believe we were out of that trap for good. It was a great feeling of liberation, because at last I was free to quit teaching and fulfill what I believe is my only function in life: to write books."

> —*Playboy*, June 1983

"In the review of a horror novel they'll write, 'In the tradition of Stephen King…' And I can't believe that's me they're talking about. It's very dangerous to look at that too closely, because it may change me from what I want to be, which is just another pilgrim trying to get along."

> —*Yankee*, March 1979

"[Has success spoiled Stephen King?] Yes. Yes, it has. It has. I've turned into an utter shit in the last year and a half. I couldn't help it!"

> —*Shayol*, Winter 1982

"I guard against success, because you start to expect things, preferential treatment at hotels or concerts. I don't want that. I'm not any better than anyone else."

> —*Time*, October 6, 1986

"Probably the worst of it is that the phone rings all the time and people drive by the house and take pictures and there's a lot of mail to be answered. It seems like a lot of people want something. They want a piece of you."
—*WB*, November-December 1989

"The numbers have gotten very big.... I have times when I feel as if I planted a modest packet of words and grew some kind of magic beanstalk...or a runaway garden of books (OVER 40 MILLION KING BOOKS IN PRINT!!!!, as my publisher likes to trumpet). Or, put it another way—sometimes I feel like Mickey Mouse in *Fantasia*. I knew enough to get the brooms started, but once they started to march, things are never the same."
—*The Bachman Books*, 1985

"I started out as a writer and nothing more. I became a popular writer and have discovered that, in the scale-model landscape of the book business, at least, I have grown into a Bestsellasaurus Rex—a big, stumbling book beast that is loved when it shits money and hated when it tramples houses. I look back on that sentence and feel an urge to change it because it sounds so self-pitying; I cannot change it because it also conveys my real sense of perplexity and surprise at this absurd turn of events. I started out as a storyteller; along the way I became an economic force, as well."
—*Castle Rock*, July 1985

"That sounds totally conceited, but I don't mean it that way: I can lose half of my fan base and still have enough to live on very comfortably. I've had the freedom to follow my own course, which is great. I might have lost some fans, but I might've gained some too."
—*The Paris Review*, Fall 2006

§

THE SUPERNATURAL
AND OTHER PHENOMENA

"I've never even attended a séance. Jesus, no! Precisely because I know a little bit about the subject, that's the last thing I'd ever do. You couldn't drag me to one of those things, and the same thing goes for a Ouija board. All that shit—stay away from it! Sure, I know most mediums are fakes and phonies and con artists... But if there are things floating around out there—disembodied entities, spirit demons, call them what you will—then it's the height of folly to invite them to use you as a channel into this world. Because they might like what they found, man, and they might want to stay!"
　　　—*Playboy*, June 1983

"I would not participate [in a séance] under any circumstances. Not even if my wife died and a medium said she had a message from my wife. I cannot conceive of circumstances under which I would participate in that sort of thing or stay overnight in a house that was reputed to be haunted or any of those things. We are too close as it is to a world that is incomprehensible. And the time comes when you and I and everyone who walks the face of this earth has to walk that world. We will know then, and I can wait."
　　　—*The Highway Partrolman*, July 1987

"I do think that if there is survival, if people really do remain after death, then what's going on there is that places absorb the emotions of those individuals who have been there."
　　　—*Sounds*, May 21, 1983

"It's always been difficult for me to understand why the dead would want to hang around old deserted houses, clanking chains and groaning spectrally to frighten the passersby…if they could go elsewhere. It sounds like a drag to me."
—*Danse Macabre*, 1981

"I've never seen a ghost, but sometimes at night I'll see a pattern of shadows and I'll be convinced it tells me about the later stages of existence. Or there's the textured quality of dreams. What other worlds do they come from?"
—*The Observer*, August 9, 1998

"I go see a movie like *Amityville* in New York, and there's this kind of respectful silence and you look and you say to yourself, 'The Church of Times Square is now in session.' Because these people are trying to touch something that's supernatural or beyond the bounds of ordinary rational, empirical life as they know it, but they're trying to touch it in a very secular way, in a way that sort of short-circuits ideas of God, the devil, Satanism, all that stuff."
—*Miami Herald*, March 25, 1984

"If people ask me if I even believe in psychic phenomenon, my answer is I think that I do. There seems to be enough evidence to suggest that something like that's going on, but I don't think about it that much."
—*Inside*, April 4, 1986

"The scientific verdict's still out on most of those things, and they're certainly nothing to accept as an article of faith. But I don't think we should dismiss them out of hand just because we can't as yet understand how and why they operate and according to what rules. There's a big and vital difference between the unexplained and the inexplicable, and we should keep that in mind when discussing so-called psychic phenomena."
—*Playboy*, June 1983

"I am interested in [ESP] and I think now in the latter half of the twentieth century we have enough documentation so that anyone that doubts the psychic experience is an actual empiric reality is on the level with a person who continues to smoke two or three packs of cigarettes a day and denies that there is a link between smoking and lung cancer. The documentation is there. It can barely be questioned any further. We have as much proof, furthermore, barring some technological development that does not exist now, as we are ever going to have. It is simply the preponderance of evidence; it precludes the doubt almost entirely."

—*The Highway Patrolman*, July 1987

"I tend to believe that a lot of what goes on in the psychic world—well, let's put it this way, that most of it is either the work of knowing charlatans or people who are being misled by their own needs, their own psychological make-up. But some of it defies that easy explanation, so I'm an agnostic who leans toward belief."

—"Probabilities," September 8, 1979

"We've got appropriations in this country right now for psychic research. But when they say 'psychic research,' they're not really interested in psychic research. They're interested in producing experts who can read thoughts so they can chuck this guy over to Czechoslovakia or somewhere, where he can tell us where the silos are and that sort of thing, simply by reading thoughts."

—*High Times*, January 1981

§

TV

"*Route 66* raised the consciousness of every white kid in America. You found out there was a different way to live than taking college courses and getting out and going nine to five. And what have my kids got? *B.J. and the Bear.*"
—*Penthouse*, April 1982

"[On Rod Serling:] The first couple of years you're looking at the work of a man who was just entranced with the idea that he didn't have to be totally realistic in every way. The first two years—and they were the best—were the work of a man drunk on fantasy."
—*Twilight Zone*, December 1985

"[C]onsidering the limitations of TV, *Salem's Lot* could have turned out a lot worse than it did. The two-part TV special was directed by Tobe Hooper of *Texas Chainsaw Massacre* fame, and outside of a few boners—such as making my vampire Barlow look exactly like the cadaverously inhuman night stalker in the famous German silent film *Nosferatu*—he did a pretty good job. I breathed a hearty sigh of relief, however, when some plans to turn it into a network series fell apart, because today's television is just too institutionally fainthearted and unimaginative to handle real horror."
—*Playboy*, June 1983

"TV is death to horror. When [*Salem's Lot*] went to TV a lot of people moaned and I was one of the moaners."
—*Bangor Daily News*, November 17, 1979

"[On *Salem's Lot*:] Sure, it probably would have been better if it wasn't done for television, but I'm not gonna run around screaming 'They wrecked my fuckin' book!'"
—*Famous Monsters*, April 1980

"I have been offered a series seven times by various networks. I have turned the offers down, partly because it's not a good time for such a project for me personally, and partly because I feel to do horror well, you have to have some freedom, which television doesn't give you because of the restrictions imposed by the 'standards and practice' laws, which is basically censorship."
—*Footsteps*, November 1986

"I'd tell these people, 'You are in a position now where you can't show somebody getting punched in the nose more than once in one hour of primetime television, and you want to put horror on TV?' My reaction was that I didn't want to do it simply because I didn't want to be on TV for six weeks and then be axed because everybody tuned out when they found out there was nothing there to watch!"
—*Famous Monsters*, April 1980

"*The Wire* keeps getting better, and to my mind it has made the final jump from great TV to classic TV—put it right up there with *The Prisoner* and the first three seasons of *The Sopranos*. It's the sort of dramatic cycle people will still be writing and thinking about 25 years from now, and given the current state of the world and the nation, that's a good thing. 'There,' our grandchildren will say. 'It wasn't all Simon Cowell.'"
—*Entertainment Weekly*, September 1, 2006

"Am I putting TV viewers down, accusing them of being dumb? I am not. You come home tired, you want something that's fun and familiar? That's fine. It doesn't preclude the thrill of discovering something new—just look at the success of *24*. All I'm saying is that inertia is a tough barrier to crash through, and *Kingdom Hospital* wasn't capable of doing it. Those last four episodes sure are fine, though—for me, they pay off like a jackpot in Vegas. I only wish I could have brought a larger audience along to collect it."
—*Entertainment Weekly*, July 9, 2004

"At least I've never gotten hooked on the so-called 'reality shows.' I do make-believe for a living, and I know it when I see it. *Extreme Makeover? The Apprentice? Survivor?* Mother, please. These shows, which specialize in blurring the line between fact and fiction, are entertainment only a James Frey junkie could love."

—*Entertainment Weekly*, March 31, 2006

"The whole issue of violence in TV and movies boils down to, 'Are we telling the truth about human nature as we know it?' I'm trying to be moral. I don't want to lie about what people would do in certain circumstances. And if I do, I run the risk of glamorizing violence."

—*The Philadelphia Inquirer*, April 2, 1994

"[C]onsider the three great lessons history teaches us: Those who do not learn from the past are condemned to repeat it; most politicians are psychologically incapable of practicing what they preach; and when it comes to TV, the term 'creative development' is an oxymoron."

—*Entertainment Weekly*, July 12, 2009

§

WRITING

"I had some running battles with those teachers in college who sneered at the popular fiction I carried around all the time. They'd go around all day with essentially unreadable books like *Waiting for Godot*. I was their court jester. 'Oh, King, he's got some peculiar notions about writing,' they'd say."
  —*Yankee*, March 1979

"Most fiction-writers are schizophrenic by nature. Which makes us crazy, I suppose, but it's a profitable madness."
  —StephenKing.com, September 4, 2008

"You do have to be a little nuts to be a writer at all because you have to imagine worlds that aren't there. You're hearing voices, you're making believe, you're doing all of the things that we're told as children not to do. Writers don't outgrow that. If you look at writers' faces, they have young faces, child faces, especially around the eyes. And it's because they spend their life making believe. And all the kids who read *Writing* magazine know about the play yard; some of them still go there. But [adults] like me...we still get to go to the play yard. From 8 a.m. to 12 noon every day, I get to go to the play yard. I sit there and I get to make believe. That's what I do, and they pay me to do it!"
  —*Writing!*, October 2005

"[W]riting is like a little hole in reality that you can go through and you can get out and you can be someplace else for a while."
  —"An Evening with Stephen King at the Billerica," 1983

"The reason I write this stuff is a sense of wonder, a sense that there could be something more, or there's a way to establish the world and the natural laws that govern the world."
　　　　　—Speech in Truth or Consequences, New Mexico,
　　　　　　November 19, 1983

"I've never considered myself a blazingly original writer in the sense of conceiving totally new and fresh plot ideas. Of course, in both genre and mainstream fiction, there aren't really too many of those left, anyway, and most writers are essentially reworking a few basic themes, whether it's the angst-ridden introspection and tiresome identity crises of the aesthetes, the sexual and domestic problems of the John Updike school of cock contemplators, or the traditional formulas of mystery and horror and science fiction."
　　　　　—*Playboy*, June 1983

"I don't believe in the idea that a symbol or theme should be coded so that only college graduates can read it. The only thing that type of self-conscious literature is good for is for people to dissect it and use it to get graduate degrees or write doctoral theses."
　　　　　—*Twilight Zone*, February 1984

"All my life as a writer I have been committed to the idea that in fiction the story value holds dominance over every other facet of the writer's craft; characterization, theme, mood—none of those things is anything if the story is dull. And if the story does hold you, all else can be forgiven."
　　　　　—*Night Shift* (Foreword), 1977

"If a writer like me has any value at all, then I think what I'm supposed to say are things that other people either don't dare to say or find embarrassing. They say to themselves, 'But if I say that, what will people think of me?'"
　　　　　—*Sounds*, May 21, 1983

"This is a short book because most books about writing are filled with bullshit. Fiction writers, present company included, don't understand very much about what they do—not why it works when it's good, not why it doesn't when it's bad. I figured the shorter the book, the less the bullshit."
　　　　　—*On Writing* (Second Foreword), 2000

"To me even after 35 years—most of my life—of writing stories, the process itself is a total mystery. I have no idea how creativity happens or what it does to the person who creates it except that it makes you feel good while it's going on."
—*Lilja's Library*, February 20, 2008

"The act of writing stories hasn't been new for me in a long time, but that doesn't mean it's lost its fascination. If I don't find ways of keeping it fresh and interesting, though, it'll get old and tired in a hurry. I don't want that to happen, because I don't want to cheat the people who read my stuff (that would be you, dear Constant Reader), and I don't want to cheat myself, either. We're in it together, after all. This is a date we're on. We should have fun. We should dance."
—*Everything's Eventual* (Introduction), 2001

"[C]haracters get away sometimes and they start to go on their own and all you can do is hope that they go in a place that won't make the book too uncomfortable for you. You don't always know what's going to happen."
—"Probabilities," September 8, 1979

"I never plot out beforehand. I have a general story idea...a given situation. If you start to lie, then things wander off course. That is, if you start to make characters do things because it would be more convenient for you."
—*Read*, October 21, 2005

"[Y]ou make an agreement with yourself: You say: 'Within those wide limitations of character, let them do whatever's realistic.' And don't you stop them if they're doing something you don't like, because you will like it if you really watch it and let it happen."
—*Writer's Digest*, March 1992

"The voice of a story (usually third person, sometimes first person) always comes with the package. So does the form an idea will take. I feel most comfortable writing novels, but I also write short stories, screenplays, and the occasional poem. The idea always dictates the form. You can't make a novel be a short story, you can't make a short story be a poem, and you can't stop a short story that decides it wants to be a novel instead (unless you want to kill it, that is)."
—*Storm of the Century* (Introduction), 1999

"[M]y interest has always been in telling stories. The stories themselves may be unbelievable. But within the framework of the stories I'm concerned that what people do in those stories should be as real as possible and that the characters of the people should be as real as possible."
—*Miami Herald*, March 25, 1984

"I don't really map anything out. I just let it happen. But once it happens, it's always there. If it's laid, it's played. If I get to page 300 and it's not working, I junk it. But it's just paper..."
—*Entertainment Weekly*, December 1, 2006

"The job of the writer is to impose order on chaos, to create the necklace we call 'story' from the various unstrung beads of ideas, images, character, tone, mood."
—*Whispers*, August 1982

"The novelist is, after all, God's liar, and if he does his job really well, keeps his head and his courage, he can sometimes find the truth that lives at the center of the lie."
—*Danse Macabre*, 1981

"I can keep five to seven major characters in my mind... But I think you should try and stick with two or three, unless you're a genius, somebody like Paul Scott, who wrote *The Raj Quartet*. It's very difficult to keep a number of real complex central characters in your mind. But when it comes to secondary characters, I can hold as many as 30 together without too much trouble, because they tend to be these sort of Dickensian characters; they're very eccentric and colorful. I like them a lot and so they're easy to remember."
—*Writer's Digest*, March 1992

"I don't always intend to do horror, but somehow things almost always head that way. If they don't, I'm not going to fight it. You go where you feel you have to go. Writing is like that. You can't always tell yourself you're going to write one particular thing and that's that. You get the story, and the story takes hold, and away you go."
—*Twilight Zone*, April 1981

"Although 'Where do you get your ideas?' has always been the question I'm most frequently asked (it's number one with a bullet, you might say), the runner-up is undoubtedly this one: 'Is horror all you write?' When I say it isn't, it's hard to tell if the questioner seems relieved or disappointed."
—*Different Seasons* (Afterword), 1982

"I write for an audience of one, and that's me. One of the things you have to think about when you're a success on a large level is, if you write for yourself, if you write for that audience of one, you must have some kind of a mind to write right in the middle of everything. And you must be like Mr. Average, at the bottom. I enjoy writing things that either scare me, or if they don't scare me, I know they're going to scare the audience. I know that it's gonna get you."
—*Larry King Live*, April 10, 1986

"I would advise any writer trying to achieve success to ignore popular fashion as much as possible and write about what he or she really wants to write. Of course, it helps to remember that writing is an act of communication. The more accessible your work is, the more people will want to read it."
—*Cosmopolitan*, December 1985

"I used to tell interviewers that I wrote every day except for Christmas, the Fourth of July, and my birthday. That was a lie. I told them that because if you agree to an interview you have to say something, and it plays better if it's something at least half-clever. Also, I didn't want to sound like a workaholic dweeb (just a workaholic, I guess). The truth is that when I'm writing, I write every day, workaholic dweeb or not."
—*On Writing*, 2000

"For me, if there's pain sometimes it's when I come in to start a new day and I sit down and say, 'I gotta pick up this fish again and it's rotted some more and I've got to smell it.' It's tough to get going, but there can be times, completely the opposite of pain, when suddenly you'll feel this burst of exhilaration when suddenly you see something with perfect clarity."
—*The Author Talks: Stephen King*, 1987

"Usually, in the afternoon, I have what I call my 'toy truck,' a story that might develop or might not, but meanwhile it's fun to work on. Sometimes it's a story and sometimes it's a novel that might germinate. I begin to pile up some pages, and eventually it'll get shifted over to the morning."
    —*Twilight Zone*, April 1981

"I don't even write a lot. I just sort of write every day and keep it rolling along. I think a lot of writers have a tendency to stand back awhile and sort of sniff around a project if it's not going well."
    —*Famous Monsters*, April 1980

"A story or a novel is, after all, only a chain of coherent imaginative thoughts tied together with occasional bursts of that mysterious nerve-lightning we call creativity."
    —*Whispers*, August 1982

"The imaginative job of keeping an ambitious piece of work rolling not just over years but decades is immense. Self-doubt is part of any creative effort, but at least you get a break from it if you're working on a single novel or movie; when you're slowly building a series, self-doubt settles in as a houseguest and greets you every morning in its robe and slippers. After a while it even starts making the coffee. 'Hey, how ya doin'?' it asks. 'How you gonna screw up today? And oh, by the way, you've been doing this five years now—want to go for 10?'"
    —*Entertainment Weekly*, July 8, 2005

"John Grisham, of course, knows lawyers. What you know makes you unique in some other way. Be brave. Map the enemy's positions, come back, tell us all you know. And remember that plumbers in space is not such a bad setup for a story."
    —*On Writing*, 2000

"I took it very much to heart in college when someone said to me: write what you know. I always understood that to mean: You can go ahead and use your imagination to the very limits of its capability, but you'd better have a framework you can understand. I would feel pretty damn silly setting a novel in Los Angeles. I've been there four times in my life. And I wouldn't even dare go to Canada for a setting."
    —*Ottawa Citizen*, March 15, 2003

"I've written all these books about Maine simply because it's what I know. You have to know where the roads go and what the names of the plants are..."
—*Time*, January 17, 2008

"I hardly ever research anything unless I absolutely have to, and I've gotten a little bit more paranoid about that. It's okay to go pretty much on your imagination if a lot of people aren't reading you, but once it piles up to the point where I am right now, if you screw up anything, somebody knows. I've gotten my hands burned a couple of times."
—*Writer's Digest*, March 1992

"If you want to write and you want to write well, do it a lot. Practice it the same way you would practice anything else that you love. Get better. Work at it. Feel comfortable with it. Feel comfortable with sentences; feel comfortable with paragraphs until those things just roll off your fingertips. And the better you feel about it, the better it's going to go for you. Baseball players know about it, trombone players know about it, swimmers know about it. Use it or lose it."
—*Writing!*, October 2005

"I think we all plagiarize each other subconsciously, but there are still enough differences to make it interesting."
—*Famous Monsters*, April 1980

"I think that writers are made instead of born. I think that there are a lot of people beyond the number of people that become writers who have the talent to become writers but people underrate the amount of determination and work it takes to hone the ability where you're good enough to be read in a kind of mass market way."
—"Probabilities," September 8, 1979

"I think talent as a writer is hard-wired in, it's all there, at least the basic elements of it. You can't change it any more than you can choose whether to be right handed or left handed."
—*The Guardian*, September 14, 2000

"The biggest part of writing successfully is being talented, and in the context of marketing, the only bad writer is one who doesn't get paid."
—*Writer*, July 1986

"If I write about things, then I don't have to worry about them. You know what I mean? This is the best gig in the world, I can't even tell you, because other people pay like eighty bucks an hour to go to a shrink—and it's not even a full hour, it's a fifty-minute hour. I write these things down and people pay me. It's great! It's wonderful! People say to me, 'Do you have bad dreams?' And the answer is yes—when I don't write, then I get bad dreams."
    —Q&A in Portland, Oregon, November 2, 2006

"Other guys go to psychiatrists and pay a lot of dough to lie on an imitation leatherette couch and spout on about all their crazy terrors and weird ideas. Well, I get to do all that in my books and I get paid for it. It's sort of like expiation, if you will. It's a marketable obsession."
    —*Knave*, 1987

"[W]riting is a great job, no heavy lifting, though the pay for most writers isn't that great, but still, hey, it's fine, it's fine…"
    —*The Guardian*, September 14, 2000

"It was always a pleasure to write. I can never think of a time when I just hacked something out to fulfill a contract or meet a deadline. I might have hacked things out, but it was always stuff I loved."
    —*The Guardian*, September 14, 2000

"I think of writing as an act of communication with other people, as an act of getting in touch with them. And people seem to like what I do and I have always wanted to please other people. I was raised to please people."
    —*Knave*, 1987

"I think with the best writing you actually feel the writer's joy, the writer's vision, or something like that. God, it's a strange way to make a living. It's a child's activity, really."
    —*The Author Talks: Stephen King*, 1987

"Writing is like a twitch. You do it because you have to do it. And it's fun, God knows it's fun. All these writers say, 'Oh, it's so hard, it's such torture,' because they're having such a good time and if they told people that they'd get lynched."
    —"Turning the Thumbscrews on the Reader," 1987

"I've occasionally gone back to longhand—with *Dreamcatcher* and with *Bag of Bones*—because I wanted to see what would happen. It changed some things. Most of all, it made me slow down because it takes a long time. Every time I started to write something, some guy up here, some lazybones is saying, Aw, do we have to do that? I've still got a little bit of that scholar's bump on my finger from doing all that longhand. But it made the rewriting process a lot more felicitous. It seemed to me that my first draft was more polished, just because it wasn't possible to go so fast. You can only drive your hand along at a certain speed. It felt like the difference between, say, rolling along in a powered scooter and actually hiking the countryside."
　　—*The Paris Review*, Fall 2007

"When I've written a particularly spooky scene, I feel a great pleasure and have been known to chuckle with glee. A novelist must arouse the emotion of a reader—whether it's laughter or tears or tension."
　　—*Cosmopolitan*, December 1985

§

Writing Horror

"When I'm asked why I decided to write the sort of thing I do write, I always think the question is more revealing than any answer I could possibly give. Wrapped within it...is the assumption that the writer controls the material instead of the other way around."

      —On Writing, 2000

"I have always felt a little bit uncomfortable with that question [of why I write the kinds of stories that I write]. It's not a question that you would ask a guy that writes detective stories or the guy that writes mystery stories, or westerns, or whatever. But it is asked of the writer of horror stories because it seems that there is something nasty about our love for horror stories, or boogies, ghosts and goblins, demons and devils."

      —The Highway Patrolman, July 1987

"For some reason, nobody asks writers in the quote normal unquote fields of literary endeavor why they have chosen their particular area. If you met Joseph Heller at a cocktail party, would you ask him why he chose the Air Force for *Catch-22*?"

      —Houston Post, February 25, 1979

"Sometimes I speak before groups of people who are interested in writing or in literature, and before the question-and-answer period is over, someone always rises and asks this question: Why do you choose to write about such gruesome

subjects? I usually answer this with another question: Why do you assume that I have a choice?"
—*Night Shift* (Foreword), 1977

"The thing about this field—if you visualize American Literature as a town, then the horror writer's across the tracks on the poor side of town, and that's where 'nice' people won't go."
—*Twilight Zone*, April 1981

"The [photographer] says, 'You want to get in that coffin?' I says, 'No, I'm not going to get in that coffin. Just take a picture.' He says, 'Why don't you want to get in that coffin? You write horror stories, don't you?' I said, 'That's right, I write horror stories. If you had Louis Gossett, Jr., here, would you want to give him a piece of watermelon?'"
—*Boston Herald*, July 27, 1986

"You can call me anything you like, but I've always been a fairly subversive horror writer. I remember doing an interview about eight years ago, just after *Salem's Lot*, when the lady interviewing me said, 'As a horror writer, do you think...' and then she stopped and kind of recalled it and said 'Oh, do you mind?' It was as though she had said, 'As a nigger, oh sorry, as a black...' And I said no, you can call me anything you like."
—*Knave*, 1987

"I've been writing horror stories since I was ten years old. I'd done other stuff, but the stuff that came through with some force was the horror."
—*Twilight Zone*, April 1981

"Another reason that I've always written horror is because it's a kind of psychological protection. ... If you write a novel where the bogeyman gets somebody else's children, maybe they'll never get your own children."
—"An Evening with Stephen King at the Billerica," 1983

"By writing a horror novel where the inexplicable disorder takes over in our ordered lives, you make order look better by comparison. But below that, there's a part of us that responds to The Who bashing their instruments to pieces on the stage. There's a very primitive part that says, 'Do it some more.'"
—*High Times*, January 1981

"I've been able to talk about the American way of death in *Pet Sematary*. I've been able to talk, in another book I'm working on, about American business and American consumerism. The interesting thing is you can take these things to their furthest limit just by introducing a little bit of nightmare."
—*Los Angeles Herald*, January 31, 1989

"I do consider myself a horror writer, because I love to frighten people. Just as Garfield says, 'Lasagna is my life,' I can say, in all truth, that horror is mine. I'd write the stuff even if I weren't paid for it because I don't think there's anything sweeter on God's green earth than scaring the living shit out of people."
—*Playboy*, June 1983

"I like the idea of somebody getting really scared and sleeping with the lights on and that sort of thing. I like the sensation of power involved."
—*Sounds*, May 21, 1983

"Occasionally, somebody will say to me, 'I got a nightmare from reading your book,' and my immediate reaction is 'Serves you right for reading it.' Because when you get to the bottom of everything, what I'm involved in is trying to scare the bejeesus out of people."
—*Yankee*, March 1979

"Scaring people, especially in our day and time, is one of the hardest things on earth, as far as I am concerned. You and I and everyone else in this world live in what is probably the most difficult times that have ever been. We are facing total thermonuclear destruction; and, if you can make someone believe in a ghost or a demon or a vampire in the face of that, you are doing well."
—*The Highway Patrolman*, July 1987

"The job of a fantasy writer, or the horror writer, is to provide a single, powerful spectacle for that third eye. If I can scare my reader and keep him turning the pages, I have succeeded in my craft."
—*Cosmopolitan*, December 1985

"[T]error is the best of emotions, the best of the low emotions. That's what Poe said, and he's right and if I can get terror I will and if not, I'll go to horror, and if I can't succeed on the level of horror, I'll try to gross people out."
—"Probabilities," September 8, 1979

"[T]he horror writer always brings the bad news: you're going to die, he says; he's telling you to never mind Oral Roberts and his 'something good's going to happen to you,' because something bad is also going to happen to you, and it may be cancer and it may be a stroke, and it may be a car accident, but it's going to happen. And he takes your hand and enfolds it in his own, and he takes you into the room and he puts your hands on the shape under the sheet...and tells you to touch it here...here...and here..."
—*Night Shift* (Foreword), 1977

"I don't think that horror fiction works—I don't think it's possible to scare a person, particularly in a novel—unless you are talking in two voices: on one level, in a very loud voice, you are screaming at your audience. You are screaming about ghosts, you are screaming about werewolves, you are screaming about shape-changers, vampires, whatever. But in another, very low voice—a whisper—you are talking about real fears, so that in the best cases, you are trying to achieve that nightmare feeling that we've all had; that we know it's not real, but that doesn't matter anymore. When I can get that, I know I've got people right where I want them."
—*The Stephen King Story*, 1991

"The most important thing about building suspense is building identification with the character. You have to take some time and make your reader care about the characters in the story. I'm thinking about *Misery*, where you've got this writer, Paul Sheldon, and little by little you get to know this guy and understand him and you get to see different aspects of him. Then you start to empathize with him and you start to put yourself in his shoes and then you start to be very, very afraid because you don't want anything bad to happen to him. But because it's the kind of story that it is, you know that something bad is gonna happen. So one by one you close off the exits and things get more and more nerve-racking until finally there's an explosion."
—*Writing!*, October 2005

"First you create people that you want to live, then you put them into the cooker."
—*Time*, October 6, 1986

"[T]he thing about good horror fiction is that there can't be any horror without a little love. There can't be any darkness without light. Unless you give people a contrast, it's all—it's useless. It's like the *Friday the 13th* movies, where you have, you know, X number of young teenagers who are just there to be killed."
—*Larry King Live*, April 10, 1986

"All writers have a pipeline which goes down into the subconscious. But the man or woman who writes horror stories has a pipeline that goes further, maybe...into the sub-subconscious, if you like."
—*Time*, October 6, 1986

"Another question I get is, 'Are you ever going to write something serious?' My answer is: 'Everything I do is serious.'"
—*Houston Post*, February 25, 1979

"I love the genre, and while I may occasionally depart from it, I'll never entirely leave it. I have no set plan of design for the future—I write what seems right, what occurs."
—*Footsteps*, November 1986

"I'm running the ghost, which is more fun than being the ghost. I know where all the trapdoors are that people are going to fall into."
—*Twilight Zone*, April 1981

"I write fantasies, but draw from the world I see. If that sometimes hurts, it's because the truth usually does. John Steinbeck was accused of gratuitous ugliness when he wrote about the migration of the Okies to California in *The Grapes of Wrath*, even of trying to foment a domestic revolution, but most of his accusers—like those who made similar accusations against Upton Sinclair when he wrote about the corrupt putrescence of the meat-packing industry in *The Jungle*—were people who preferred fairy tales and happily-ever-afters. Sometimes the truth of how we live is just ugly, that's all. But to turn aside from these truths out of some perceived delicacy, or to give in to the idea that writing about violence causes violence, is to embrace hypocrisy. In Washington, hypocrisy breeds politicians. In the arts, it breeds pornography.
—VEMA keynote address, May 26, 1999

§

www.ingramcontent.com/pod-product-compliance
Lightning Source LLC
Chambersburg PA
CBHW051839020726
47502CB00005B/1857